PIMLICO

155

DECEIVED WITH KINDNESS

Angelica Garnett was born at Charleston, her parents'
home in Sussex, on Christmas Day, 1918. As a young
woman she studied acting before turning to painting,
drawing, illustration and decoration. In 1942 she
married David Garnett, who was twenty-six years her
senior (and who died in 1981), and they had four
daughters. She now lives in the south of France.

Angelica Garnett
2008

DECEIVED
WITH KINDNESS

A Bloomsbury Childhood

ANGELICA GARNETT

PIMLICO

To My Guardian Angel

PIMLICO
An imprint of Random House
20 Vauxhall Bridge Road, London SW1V 2SA

Random House Australia (Pty) Limited
20 Alfred Street, Milsons Point, Sydney
New South Wales 2061, Australia

Random House New Zealand Limited
18 Poland Road, Glenfield
Auckland 10, New Zealand

Random House (Pty) Limited
Isle of Houghton, Corner of Boundary Road & Carse O'Gowrie
Houghton 2198, South Africa

Random House Publishers India Private Limited
301 World Trade Tower, Hotel Intercontinental Grand Complex
Barakhamba Lane, New Delhi 110 001, India

The Random House Group Limited Reg. No. 954009

First published by Chatto & Windus 1984
Pimlico edition, with a new preface, 1995

11

Printed and bound in Great Britain by
Mackays of Chatham plc, Chatham, Kent

Papers used by Random House are natural,
recyclable products made from wood grown in sustainable
forests. The manufacturing processes conform to the
environmental regulations of the country of origin

ISBN 9780712662666 (from January 2007)
ISBN 0712662669

Contents

List of Illustrations

Preface to the Pimlico Edition

If I ask myself today whether I would write this book in the same way – that is, if given the subject, I would want to say the same things, the answer is Yes – albeit differently. In the ten years since it was published I have had time to see things – above all myself – otherwise, even to grow up a little. I am also less obsessed by the personalities and relationships of my mother, father and husband, less desirous of apportioning the blame, and less mesmerised by the idea of repeating or re-living my childhood. When, a year before my father's death, at the age of 59, I began writing, I was still wrapped in the caul that had bound me all my life, from which I was only just beginning to divest myself. I by no means clearly saw what I was doing – but only knew that I had to do it. The book was therefore a therapeutic exercise, an effort to save myself from hypocrisy and pretence by creeping out into the open. By the time I had finished it both my parents were dead, but I was terribly conscious of their shadows looking over my shoulder, not accusingly, but shocked and horrified at what, with the best will in the world, they had finally produced.

It is of course the same old story, the one we all live through in different ways, of the relationship with, and separation from, our parents. In my case this was obscured by the fact that the man I married was a near contemporary of my mother and father, as well as their devoted friend and lover, so that, without enough experience to understand what might lie beneath such a situation, I became the focus of an uneasy truce – rather than a war – of which I was however the unconscious but consenting casualty.

But it is not a story of violence or achievement. And perhaps, for modern readers, it is this that is most difficult to understand. Bloomsbury believed in and largely practised intellectual tolerance, but often failed to recognise the power of the emotions or the reasoning of the heart. Fascinating and vital, they hid their feelings behind an apparent detachment that I found at that time repressive and confusing. Separated as I was from them by more than the usual generation gap, their lack of physical warmth and animal spirits had the effect of inhibiting my own, making me either excessively shy and tentative in an effort to seem more grown up than I was, or arrogant and insensitive in my consuming desire to identify with them.

Brought up in the delicious climate of an Ivory Tower, I had no experience with which to counter or compare the unique one of being a spoiled, and apparently much loved child. Many years later, after Vanessa's death, I remember being assured by Raymond Mortimer that I *had* been much loved: and of course everyone thought so, including me. But I wonder whether a parent's love ought not to be tougher and stronger, more concerned with the relationship the child will eventually have with the world it inhabits and the common strengths, failings and emotions of its fellow inhabitants? Alienated by lack of experience, I remained both ignorant and afraid of these things, ill at ease and therefore constantly tempted to pretend.

Accusation and blame, however, are dreary props for the ego. I am convinced that, had I confronted my parents while they were still alive, in spite of any momentary pain and incomprehension, both they and I would have had a happier relationship. I cannot excuse myself for this omission, which I now see so clearly was my business and not theirs. If my marriage was an act of rebellion, it was ill-judged – and, moreover, I knew it at the time but failed to listen to the still, small but terrifying voice within. It was this failure and deadly suppression which coloured my marriage rather than David's own personality, and it was also necessary to recognise that, together with my resentment, I must discard the self-protective role of eternal victim.

Writing it out, that is to say committing myself to a definite point of view, seemed to hold the promise of exorcism. The effort I had to make to re-live my experience helped me define my attitude and indeed my self, and was, moreover, the only way that remained, given the fact that the other protagonists were all dead. But there were many moments when I wondered whether what I was saying was justifiable. I had known these extraordinary people from a child's point of view, immeasurably different from that of a contemporary, and I allowed myself to be led by the fascination of the subject beyond these limits into a certain amount of speculation. At the time I felt that this was the only way to avoid simple nostalgia and snobbism, the latter not only a trap for the writer but for the public, always liable to over-identify with the members of an élite. Bloomsbury was the matrix from which I sprang, in many ways an extraordinary advantage: but I wished I could have called it by another name, and rechristened its characters, so that they might be seen for their psychological complexities and over- lifesize personalities without the label.

Angelica Garnett
Forcalquier, 1994

It is rather ironical that the word 'power' denotes two contradictory concepts: *power of* = capacity and *power over* = domination. This contradiction, however, is of a peculiar kind. Power = domination results from the paralysis of power = capacity. '*Power over*' is the *perversion* of '*power to*' . . . Domination is coupled with death, potency with life. Domination springs from impotence and in turn reinforces it, for if an individual can force somebody else to serve him, his own need to be productive is increasingly paralysed.

Masochism is the attempt to get rid of one's individual self, to escape from freedom, and to look for security by attaching oneself to another person . . . it can be rationalised as sacrifice, duty or love . . . often masochistic strivings are so much in conflict with the parts of the personality striving for independence and freedom that they are experienced as painful and tormenting.

Erich Fromm, *Man For Himself: An Enquiry into the Psychology of Ethics*

Les sentiments pour les progéniteurs, ça fait partie des choses qu'il vaut mieux ne pas chercher trop à tirer au clair.

André Gide, *Les Faux-Monnayeurs*

Prologue

In 1975 I was living on the north side of London in Islington, a prey to loneliness and regret, following a love affair with someone much younger than myself. My lover had gone abroad, leaving me without news of any kind, and I spent many months of doubt and anxiety before compelling myself to admit that he would never return. My children had by that time left home, and my husband, David Garnett (called Bunny by myself and our friends), from whom I had separated several years earlier, lived in France. Now I found myself alone in one of those tall London houses, with nine empty rooms, not so much unhappy as disorientated.

What else had I ever been, however, in spite of a longing to prove the contrary? I had friends, of course, but I did not feel particularly close to any of them. Either they were friends of my youth with whom the links had become attenuated by time and a change of interests, or they were those of an older generation who were friends of mine mainly because they had known and loved my parents. With them I always felt secure, but also ill at ease, sensing that there was some profound inadequacy in me to which, in their kindness, they did not allude. Our relations were inhibited either because we could not achieve a sufficient intimacy together, or because I imagined that I had nothing to offer our friendship.

An extract from a diary kept at that time indicates my lack of self-confidence, the depth and importance of which I was only just becoming aware.

London *1975*
While buying vegetables in the Caledonian Road I looked in a mirror and saw a vagueness, almost a hole, where I myself should

I

have been. Compared with the woman next to me I seemed unsure, tentative, and wispy. Yet I was better looking, better dressed, even in better health. It was not that I was daydreaming, I was simply not present in the same sort of way. I often see something indefinable in the faces of those I meet in shops or public places that reflects my non-being; and then because I smile and am anxious to please they are reassured. It's obvious after all that I'm not an escaped lunatic.

Preoccupied with myself as I was, I began to be aware of the profound and disturbing emotions I felt for my mother, Vanessa Bell, and my father, Duncan Grant. I was beginning to question their behaviour towards me.

In 1961, when she was eighty-one and I was forty-two, my mother died. Her image and personality had always obsessed me: on the one hand I felt compelled to imitate her, while on the other I resented her dominance. With Duncan I had had a different relationship: light and easy, affectionate and undemanding. I had always adored him and was quite uncritical – in my eyes he could do no wrong. But recently I had become aware of currents beneath the surface, of unsatisfied desires and longings which, partly because I did not know what they meant and partly because Duncan himself seemed so unaware, had become deeply repressed. I found it impossible to talk to him of such things.

Writing my diary proved helpful, for it provided a means of increasing my insight. Then another lifeline was held out to me by a young American called Frank Hallman, who wrote asking for permission to publish an article by my aunt, Virginia Woolf, and subsequently a memoir by Vanessa. At first we carried on a lively correspondence, and later in the summer he arrived in England. He was young, intelligent and sensitive, with a sense of humour. We liked each other immediately, a feeling which on my side was all the warmer because I hoped that here at last was that particular kind of intimacy for which I longed. I did not fall in love, but something in his manner affected me like an elixir; I was both stimulated and warmed by his evident affection. It was a reflection of what he felt for my mother, for whom he had conceived an enormous admiration. He had seen pictures by both her and Duncan in New York, but unlike most people, he had responded more strongly to Vanessa than to Duncan. It was Frank who dropped into my mind the idea that Duncan was not necessarily as attractive to everyone as he appeared to me, and that his imperfections, once realised, might make him both more interesting and more accessible.

Before returning to the States, Frank suggested that I might write a short book about Charleston – the house near Lewes in Sussex where I was born and brought up – and the life we lived there, but I resisted the idea strongly. He evidently imagined sketches of childhood, cameolike portraits of the remarkable people who had surrounded me. But I saw that even to produce these I would be forced into an involvement, from which in fact I had never been free, with the question of my relationship with Duncan and Vanessa. Already I was afraid of the effort it would cost me, of adventuring into the disturbing perspectives of the past.

Since Vanessa's death, Duncan had lived on in the country at Charleston. I often went down to see him, making the two-and-a-half-hour journey by car, assuming, much in the way small children do, that I should always be welcome. Undemonstrative though he was, Duncan never made me feel otherwise, and in that place and in his presence I had the sensation, a false one as it turned out, of being a whole and integrated person. Probably because it was not a genuine feeling, I could seldom if ever paint when I was at Charleston, an inability made all the more painful by the familiar sight of the works of art all over the house. In consequence I took more and more to gardening. I loved the walled garden with its ancient apple trees and cottage flowers, but I never felt satisfied with my weeding and pruning, and was pursued by a spectre of perfection which was both unattainable and unnecessary; added to my other feelings, it made me both grumpy and taciturn. Every day I saw Duncan slowly ageing in front of his easel, dedicated to his painting and responding happily to a host of faithful admirers, while I, rigid with suppressed love and a misery in which there was more than a tinge of jealousy, suffered from his obvious lack of interest in my life.

He was by now very old and, unable to live alone, was looked after devotedly by the poet Paul Roche, a friend of long standing, who filled the house with his grown-up children and their companions. Like a circle of butterflies they fluttered round Duncan, sometimes delighting in him, sometimes ignoring him, while he, confined to a wheel-chair, looked on them all from a distance. Provided he could continue to paint, which he was at the time doing very well, he preferred to remain detached, apparently unconcerned with what went on around him, although an occasional spark of life showed he was not as oblivious as he seemed. He lived, more than anyone I have ever known, in the present, whereas I had one foot buried in the past and, even though I didn't live at Charleston, found it difficult to accept the youthful invasion. Like a rapid current, it swept past me to occupy spaces which I had regarded as particularly my own.

Mistakenly, I clung to a certain authority there which Paul quite naturally resented, a situation which led to a sharp correspondence between us. In my diary I tried to sort out some of my emotions.

London 1975

Perhaps it's Paul's letter that has depressed me. He looks after Duncan in the most extraordinarily competent way, which, even had I the necessary physical strength, I could not do. And I think that Duncan is happy in that masculine menage which comprises the very young, the middle-aged and the very old. Paul's son, T., is a miracle of gentleness and good humour; but I can't help shrinking when they talk, as they often do, as though Duncan himself were absent, when there he is sitting at his table smiling the smile of a Taoist poet. It is shocking to think he may actually enjoy this kind of indelicacy.

4

Prologue

Paul's letter makes it clear not only that he thinks of himself as Duncan's son, but that Duncan thinks of him as the son he always wished to have. I feel murderously jealous, as though I had been given a blow in the face, although when I think of Duncan longing for a son I feel a lot of sympathy for him. It is baffling that it has taken me all these years to realise how much I resent his neglect of me, divesting himself of all responsibility, as though I were an object rather than a human being. It didn't seem like this in my childhood, when I was on the whole far happier with him than with Vanessa, because he had no axe to grind and never exercised emotional blackmail.

It has taken Paul's letter to make me aware of Duncan's feelings, and although I feel extraordinarily thick-headed not to have realised them earlier, I am glad to think that I now know Duncan better. If anything it increases my love for him. His great age makes it difficult to know what he thinks of me; it is obvious he confuses me with Vanessa – he calls me by her name, and although I know this is common in old people, I suffer a small shock every time he does it. I get the impression he cares little for me or my life, but I have to admit that I have not made it easy for him to do so.

To become aware of my jealousy of Paul was an advance, in the tangled web of repressed emotion in which I was then living.

Shortly afterwards Paul, as he sometimes did, carried Duncan off to his own house in Aldermaston where, besides other conveniences, the comfort and warmth were greater than at Charleston. This gave me an opportunity to return there alone – a visit I needed to make not only because I had begun to explore, however tentatively, my disaffection with the past, but for the purely practical reason that the house was falling into disrepair. I was worried about the future of Charleston, full as it was of paintings, decorations and objects of every kind – a testimony to the life we had lived there – and I wanted to find a way of preserving it. It had been obvious for some time that the work should be undertaken as soon as possible, but my reluctance to disturb Duncan had made it difficult to know how to begin.

I was therefore able to take advantage of Duncan's and Paul's absence to make a tour of inspection in the company of the agent and his assistant, hoping that they might persuade our landlord to repair the outside fabric. In spite of their friendliness, I discerned in their eyes a gleam of disbelief and a determination to disregard all but the solid and tangible, of which admittedly there was very little. They were visibly unmoved by the charm of the decorations, and indeed as we went round it the house seemed to shed all its qualities, like so many petals falling from a flower, to reveal the mark of damp on the walls, the holes in the roof, the plaster coming away from the wallpaper, the exposed laths filled with woodworm, etc. The imperceptible shrugs of the two men, their loaded silences, the way the agent said, 'I'm no connoisseur but . . .', my feeling that I seemed to be doing the wrong thing in showing them round, added up to something unpleasant like a drop that gathers at the end of one's nose . . .

At the time the landlord was building a disproportionately large silage and hay barn behind the old farm buildings. As yet unfinished, it was a skeleton of bolted steel girders rising above the moss-covered slates and tiles of the flint barn. A milking parlour for four hundred cows was planned for the rickyard. The white chalk road full of potholes was to be concreted, and I imagined the constant rumbling of tractors and the hum of the milking machine interposing a mechanical screen between ourselves and the sounds of the countryside. Although farming is less destructive than many other pursuits, I felt that the air of the Sleeping Beauty which then possessed Charleston would inevitably disappear. I grew more and more depressed, especially as it became clear that the rent Duncan paid was too low to justify the landlord spending anything on repairs. I knew it was right that the agent should see it, yet I felt as though I had asked him there for nothing. He could not believe that anyone would be interested in helping us to preserve it, and thought that our only chance was to put the murals in a museum. I am thankful that the agent has since been proved wrong, but at the time I suffered greatly from the fact that my defence of Charleston had been so unconvincing.

Meanwhile my correspondence with Frank Hallman continued and, in the course of his other visits to London and one to Sussex, our friendship deepened. But in the summer of 1976 the telephone rang, and a voice on the other end of the line told me that Frank, on the previous day, had dropped dead of an aneurism. Our friendship, so full of promise, was brought to a tragic end. He did not even have time to publish Vanessa's memoirs. A year later I sold my house in Islington and went to live at Charleston, from where Duncan had again departed to Aldermaston, as it turned out for the last time. I thought I could keep it going until his return in the spring, but living there again was a psychological experiment which held greater risks than I had imagined.

I loved the place and all that was in it, but there was a sense of compulsion about my return, as though this time I were going back to the cave of the enchantress, the role in which I saw Vanessa. Surrounded by the subtle and glowing colours which splashed and streaked every surface, transforming walls, mantelpieces, doors and furniture, all familiar to me from childhood, I was too close to see things dispassionately, and yet I could not tear myself away. I moved about the house as in a dream, aware of the atmosphere distilled by the vibrant colours and yet hardly seeing them, preoccupied with the effort of imagining Duncan and Nessa in their early years, youthful as I had never known them. I felt as though I had a debt to pay – and yet, on reflection, I had begun to wonder whether the debt was mine or theirs.

Obscurely, I felt it necessary to come to terms with them in a place where I had spent a large part of my childhood and which I had always thought of as my home. At the same time the force of personality of both my parents, together with their philosophy or attitude to life, constituted a threat which until then I had never properly considered. My fear was that this threat, inextricably mixed with their love for me, would swamp me for ever. I was again alone, with no one to talk to and, in any case, little idea of how to describe my state of mind. Had it not been for the visits of one of my younger daughters, Fan, the experiment might have ended in disaster.

First, however, there was Duncan's ninety-third birthday party, given by Clarissa and Paul Roche at Aldermaston. I drove over there and was taken in to see Duncan in his room at one end of the house. He was very quiet and gentle, wearing his little knitted cap *à l'orientale* – absolutely himself. He asked questions about Charleston and about my daughters. Surprisingly alert, he remained personally uninvolved; he was affectionate, but I was mainly conscious of his exquisite good manners.

Friends arrived and were invited into the sitting-room. Duncan was wheeled in and people went up and spoke to him: as always, he showed himself open to new impressions. Clarissa, who is a superb cook, provided us with a delicious meal, and Duncan was served in his own corner. There were gossip, giggles and intimacy; no arguments or intellectual profundity, only towards the end (and after a lot of wine) a few personal revelations. It was the sort of occasion Duncan always enjoyed.

Duncan occupied an agreeable room full of Paul's books and his own pictures. A canary flew from cornice to cornice, or perched on Duncan's feet. A door gave on to a newly built conservatory, its roof supported by a central pillar of looking-glass, which Paul imagined would eventually be surrounded by a pool of water. Already he had filled the corners of the room with camellias and other plants. I felt as I went into it that I was stepping into a dream, a dream of the South, of perpetual sunshine and lethargy, and a little startling in our northern climate. It was hardly an interior which Duncan would have created himself, and I wondered whether he liked it. The important thing, however, was that he was still producing small paintings, which meant that he must be happy.

In the spring of 1978, about two months after his birthday, Duncan died. Not long beforehand he had returned from Paris with a chill, having been to see the great Cézanne exhibition at the Grand Palais. Staying at the British Embassy as a guest of Sir Nicholas Henderson, an old friend, Duncan fell out of bed on his last morning there and caught cold: Paul, who was with him, postponed their return for twenty-four hours and then brought him back to Aldermaston and put him to bed.

I cannot be sure how long it was after this that Paul called to tell me how Duncan was. After he rang off I suddenly realised how bad things were, and that unless I went over to Aldermaston I should probably never see him again. I suggested to my brother Quentin, who lived only three miles from Charleston, that he might like to come with me; I drove and we arrived in the afternoon. Duncan, frail as a skeleton leaf and speechless on account of his bronchitis, was nevertheless pleased to see us. He lay in bed with his cap on and with his hands, blue with cold, lying on his chest. We found ourselves in the awkward position of making conversation round someone who, though hearing and seeing, could not participate. Quentin was full of resource and knew better than to ask Duncan questions to which he could not reply. I was more or less silent. Paul kept on bringing the conversation back to the subject of who was to be the author of Duncan's biography after his death, like a child who has been told not to touch a sore spot and cannot forbear doing so.

We must have stayed for about an hour, which, though all too short, was sufficient to tire Duncan. It was indeed the last time I saw him: he was perfectly self-possessed, alive to all that was going on, gentle and remote with the distance that age confers. He never appeared to suffer, either from his physical ailments or from his necessary dependence on others. He looked like a cross between a mandarin and a gnome, and as I stared at his hands, long and narrow, I remembered how delicate and dancelike his gestures used to be.

The drive back was exhausting, but it was nice to be alone with Quentin, and I think he was as glad as I was that we had been. I was pleased that my general inertia had not prevented me from asking him to go with me.

About a fortnight later Paul rang to say that Duncan had died quietly and peacefully; just the way one expected him to go – Duncan never did anything painfully. It was decided that he should be buried beside Vanessa in Firle churchyard.

The funeral itself took place on a grey spring day. The little churchyard was very green and situated in an *au-delà-du-temps*, reminding me for some reason of the garden of the Hesperides: Paris and the Three Graces would have been welcome. As it was, there was a small crowd of friends, including our former cook and her husband, and Angus Davidson, the author and translator. He was calm, dignified and pale, the only friend from Duncan's past. A lot of people were in tears. Paul's daughter had painted the coffin with wreaths of flowers, a Pre-Raphaelite gesture that would have delighted Duncan.

After the funeral Paul and his children drove off, and the rest of us, with the exception of Quentin and his wife, went back to Charleston. We sat around the tea-table feeling purged of our petty rivalries and jealousies – or so it seemed to me; Angus's benevolence and distinction may have influenced us. Then they all went away, leaving me once more to my solitude.

Immediately after Duncan's death I began to suffer from a continuous headache. At first negligible, after a time it felt as though, when I bent my head, a set of billiard balls clashed together in the middle of my forehad. Activities such as gardening became impossible. Examinations revealed nothing and pills were useless; finally a violent pain seized the back of my neck and more or less prostrated me. As I lay in Vanessa's bedroom I had the sensation of being sucked into a vortex from which, as in a nightmare, it was imperative but impossible to escape.

Weeks went by during which no one was able to suggest what was wrong, weeks when I felt less and less capable of normal emotion. There was a moment when I thought of the pond as a solution, but Fan, who had been with me some of the time, came to the rescue when she wrote to say she thought I might die, owing to the strain of living at Charleston! This startled me into action, and I decided to move into a nursing home in London, where I was told I was suffering from a depression: a psychiatrist gave me jade green pills to swallow. I shall never forget the moment when, lying in bed in the evening, I felt an unmistakable trickle of vitality wriggle down my spine. I simply lay there, allowing this miracle to take possession of me, like an urn being filled with water.

It was a long time before I felt completely normal, but I could at least lead the life of an ordinary human being, and I returned to Charleston to an exceptionally beautiful spring, when the Japanese cherry that I had put in the year before flowered with the palest pink almond-scented blossom. The rediscovery of country life, the beauty of the downs and the garden, entranced me. In addition I felt a new freedom, and the idea of writing the book that Frank had suggested now began to take hold of me. It was a way of appreciating him, of remaining in touch with his memory, and I began to see that it might be my own way out of the labyrinth. As I thought about my childhood and adolescence I began to realise that the past may be either fruitful or a burden; that the present, if not lived to the full, may turn the past into a threatening serpent; and that relationships that were not fully explored at the time can become dark shapes, in the shadow of which we do not care to linger. To me, Vanessa had become such a shade.

When she was alive, I had seen her only as a stumbling block, as a monolithic figure who stood in my way, barring my development as a human being. Unable to wrench myself away from her for whom I had such feelings, I burdened her instead of myself with the responsibility for my life. The result was that when she died I felt almost nothing save the oppressive shadow of her presence and the faint hope that I might one day be free of it.

Why had I not revolted while there was still time, thus discovering my own self-respect and the ability to love Vanessa while she was still alive? I realised that I had never, during her lifetime, said to her, 'What does anything matter, since I love you?' Was this simply because I had been too inhibited, or because I *hadn't* loved her? In any case, now that she was no longer there it was impossible to say, but the idea that it might be possible to hold a dialogue with the dead began to form in my mind.

In the passage at Charleston I had hung some photographs of my grandmother, Julia Jackson, taken by my great-great aunt, Julia Margaret Cameron. As I looked at them I became conscious of an inheritance not only of genes but also of feelings and habits of mind which, like motes of dust spiralling downwards, settle on the most recent generation. Vanessa shrank into a mere individual in a chain of women who, whether willingly or not, had learnt certain traits, certain attitudes from one another through the years. One of these was clearly seen in a snapshot that always stood on Vanessa's writing-table, and which I now keep in the same place, of Julia in profile looking out of the window. Because of its intimacy it held a special significance for Vanessa, but for me at least half its meaning lies in its resemblance to Vanessa herself. It is not so much the physical likeness as the resemblance of gesture and intention; there is a reluctance, a hesitation in the hand raised towards the light, a doubt betrayed by the subtle and gracious lines of the pose, which links Julia and Vanessa close together. I know that I too sometimes take such poses, for example on entering a room full of people of whom I feel shy. How far back do such inheritances go? Julia's mother for instance, one of the famous and beautiful Pattle sisters, did she also suffer from lack of self-confidence? It was she whom Vanessa, as a little girl, remembered enveloped in layer upon layer of shawls. She seems to have retired early from a life that was eminently respectable and impeccably dull to spend her mature years protected by her daughter from all disturbance. Was this merely Victorian indulgence or real fragility?

Yet, as I read Vanessa's early letters to her sister and to her husband Clive, I was astonished by a vitality that I had not known was there; it was like uncovering a spring of silver water. An earlier identity glowed tantalisingly through these pages and through other people's memories and allusions, calling to life the mother I had always wanted, and with whom so many had fallen in love. Such a woman had invented the vibrant colours and shapes that surrounded me. I remembered that Bunny, who had known her well in those days, described her as full of energy – riding a bicycle, going for walks, playing with dogs and children, making jokes, a woman full of sympathy and friendliness.

It was a woman that I could see through the much darker personality of the later Vanessa, which lay far more heavily on my consciousness. I was puzzled by the fact that there seemed to be more than the usual contrast between youth and age, as though for some hidden reason the two had been deeply divided at about the time of my birth. Although it was obviously rooted in what went before it, I could not understand what had happened to colour the second half of her life less vividly. I felt intensely attracted by the younger Vanessa, and at the same time faintly uneasy: the trouble, it seemed, stemmed from my birth.

I

Vanessa

For many years I was so much a part of Vanessa, and she of me, that I could not have attempted to describe her with detachment, and even now I sometimes feel as though she might be looking over my shoulder. It is only now, and still with hesitation, that I feel I can portray her from a greater distance and affirm my separation from a personality I have spent so much time thinking about. I hope to be excused a skeleton of biographical facts without which, to my mind, her behaviour would lack meaning.

Although she eventually formed part of a society that was to have lasting influence, it was a small group within which Vanessa exerted her power, a group very susceptible to personal ascendancy. Some of its members, notably Virginia Woolf and Maynard Keynes, gained world recognition, but there was some element in Vanessa which refused to compete, restricting her energies to a more personal arena, where she reigned supreme.

She reminded me of a mountain covered with snow: at its summit the sun shone with warmth and splendour, and there was a sweetness and gaiety in the air. Further down the clouds gathered, plunging the lower, more arid slopes into darkness. At the centre of the mountain ran a deep river, glimpsed only at intervals, when it surged through a rift in the hillside with unexpected and disconcerting power.

It is strange that, given this power, Vanessa seems to have left behind her a memory less substantial than one might expect. Perhaps this is simply the effect of a complex personality difficult to define and therefore to remember, and perhaps it is also the consequence of her own reticence – her dislike of a public image. In order to understand Vanessa, one has to accept and enter her private world, a world from which she excluded all except her most cherished friends and relations, but within which she created a dazzling interior.

Vanessa was not only Virginia Woolf's sister, she was also the eldest of the Stephen family by her father Leslie's second marriage. Both her parents had been married before and both were widowed. Leslie's first wife, Minnie Thackeray, had left him with a backward daughter Laura, who was incorporated into his new family. His second wife, Julia Duckworth, a great beauty, had been passionately in love with her first husband and suffered deeply on his death: in spite of her vivacity she remained something of a tragic figure. On her marriage to Leslie she had brought with her three children by Herbert Duckworth: George, Stella and Gerald – the first two in their different ways of great importance to the Stephens.

The gap in age was considerable, however, whereas that between Vanessa and her full brothers and sister was as close as possible, as was their intimacy. Next to Vanessa came her adored brother Thoby, also of great importance in her emotional development; then Virginia who through the accident of sex was thrown together with Vanessa, for a time becoming a psychological burden of considerable proportions; and lastly Adrian who as an unwanted child was spoiled, over-protected and inhibited. According to Virginia, Vanessa felt her responsibilities towards them keenly: thrust into a maternal role by nurses and Julia alike, she had no choice but to respond, tempted by rewards of love and affection, and proud no doubt of being thought capable and worthy.

But it was Julia whose nervous energy dominated the family, leaving behind in Vanessa's mind the glow of an unattainable ideal. One evening in the bathroom, when she and Virginia were still small children, Virginia suddenly asked Vanessa whom she preferred, her father or her mother. 'Such a question seemed to me rather terrible; surely one ought not to ask it. However, I found I had little doubt as to my answer. "Mother," I said.' Vanessa had, as it were, already been inoculated with Julia's image, and in later life it was this she longed to evoke. Whenever she talked of her Vanessa's voice would take on a hint of exaltation which hid her mother's profile through the gold dust of memory, revealing a figure of such perfection that it was hardly real at all. Clearly Vanessa was profoundly moved, as only a child can be, by her mother's personality. The aura of tragedy, her distinction, her natural authority had all left an indelible mark.

In those days children saw less of their parents than they do now, and it seems that Julia was often absent from home on visits to relations. One has the impression of someone with a very firm sense of what was most important in life, valuing devotion and responsibility, only running away from them when they threatened to overcome her. She had a compelling, even dominating personality, and ran the household in a mood that may, one feels, have been a trifle tense. In spite of her underlying sadness, she could hold an audience spellbound and make them laugh. At times, she was tempted to direct the lives of others, performing charitable works and occasionally indulging in matchmaking. Anything but flirtatious or flighty, she aroused the passions of James Russell Lowell, the American author and at that time Ambassador, which were extinguished only with her death. And it was she alone who could command the obedience of J. K. Stephen, her husband's nephew, when he lost his mental equilibrium.

For Vanessa she remained a glamorous figure, authoritative and romantic, rustling in silk and for ever active, running from top to bottom of the house, or sitting, grave and concentrated, in silent communion with her husband in the drawing-room. Although she was only to know her mother for a bare fifteen years, the aura with which she surrounded Julia may have owed some of its magic to the fact that she did not survive into Vanessa's adolescence. She remained mysterious, deeply loved but scarcely understood.

After the death of Julia, and of her stepsister Stella shortly afterwards, Vanessa's sense of maternal responsibility, already forced into precocious maturity, became a vulnerable point in her make-up. Left exposed as the one who was expected to take charge of the large and – by our standards – formal household, she was obliged to account for every penny, week by week, to her persistent and guilt-ridden father.

If Leslie Stephen seemed relentless it was not because he was, in reality, insensitive or unimaginative, but with his unbalanced image of himself, he had little idea of the effect he produced on young and tender natures. Always prone to the purple passages of emotional self-indulgence, he was, in spite of the sense of proportion that emerges from his writing, thrown into an excess of self-pity by his wife's death. One must, however, remember that this was the second such occasion in his life, and that he was now well beyond middle age. As a widower he found himself face to face with duties that had previously been carried out by Julia. It was she who at his request had held the purse-strings and now, after Stella's death, and though she lacked experience, he felt that Vanessa would take charge of them. His groans of despair and peculiar system of accounting resulted from a feeling of rage that fate should aim, at this stage, to transform him into a responsible adult, and his resentment was directed against Vanessa, as the representative of her mother, who had so selfishly deserted him on the threshold of old age. But he had not reckoned on a character protected from emotional blackmail by an inner wisdom and an absent-minded dreaminess that saw through his intentions. Outwardly insulated though she was, however, Vanessa's task was no less of a burden – and these scenes left in her mind a residue of intense dislike, owing to the pain of seeing her father behave in a way she could not respect. It may have been this impression that clarified her own attitude to money; in later life she gave with generosity and never attached conditions to the gift. If this was a reaction to Leslie's hysteria, it was an admirable one.

On the whole it was only when Leslie's egotism became uppermost that he aroused feelings of antagonism. When his children were small he identified with at least some of their interests – their opinions of what they read, their sailing boats in Kensington Gardens, and their fondness for butterflies and dogs.

He observed his children's differing personalities, and as their minds developed they came to appreciate his honesty, integrity and unworldliness: whether they realised it or not they adopted many of his values. Vanessa greatly admired his rejection of Christian belief, which seemed to her both courageous and clear-headed: she admired and was seduced by the rationalist point of view, to which she accorded an importance in inverse ratio to the strength of her own emotions.

None the less, in a family that was highly articulate and self-conscious, Vanessa held herself a little apart, perhaps because she was the eldest. Her reactions were slower and more instinctive than Virginia's – possibly more so than Thoby's – and she often preferred to maintain a mute independence which impressed the more volatile Virginia with a sense of strength and responsibility. Vanessa was teased by the others for her silences but they were an indication of what lay beneath, almost like a piece of semi-opaque glass let into the floor through which, when the light was favourable, one might be lucky enough to glimpse things usually hidden. One of these was her shy determination to be a painter, the other her capacity for deep feeling, in which she herself may have found something disconcerting and even frightening. The whole cast of her mind, unenquiring and passive, was opposed to analysis: unlike Virginia, she never learnt to project the light of self-questioning onto her own behaviour. Instead she clung to a hope that all problems could be solved by rationalising them, and that there was somewhere a perfect system that would do away with threatening or painful situations.

In spite of her superiority of years and experience it was from her sister that Vanessa often felt the need to protect herself. While still a child Virginia, possessed of precocious insight, christened Vanessa 'the saint', knowing that such a nickname would embarrass Vanessa by its suggestion of disingenuous self-righteousness, one of the favourite targets of the younger members of the family. Virginia, though far from heartless, could seldom resist exhibiting her cleverness, winning for herself a reputation for brilliance as well as untrustworthiness, whereas Vanessa particularly

Vanessa, Stella and Virginia, 1896

prided herself on her reliability. It was with reservations that Vanessa showed Virginia her most intimate feelings, never sure of how they would be handed back to her, or of the form in which they might reach other people. In spite of this, however, and even in homage to her sister's insight and intelligence, it was to her that Vanessa revealed her early ambitions. On this level, even if subject to a natural sense of rivalry, Virginia's reactions were generous.

Apart from such rivalry, however, there was the unfortunate tendency, prevalent among most Stephens, to feel inadequate, not so much in the face of life as of other people. Standing beside Vanessa, Virginia felt unworthy of her, and it was perhaps specially difficult for her, strong in intellect, but weaker in the more traditional feminine qualities, to accept the part assigned them by their mother. Although their home was governed by a woman – one might say, *because* of this fact – it was organised in favour of man: in Julia's mind women were, if not slaves, doomed to serve their better halves. Her daughter Stella, who adored her, led the life of a nun, crushed and subservient – and had Julia survived she would have undoubtedly taken it for granted that her other two daughters should put love and service first. As it was, practically uneducated, and considered to be of less importance than their brothers, who were sent to boarding school, they remained at home. Vanessa, the more domesticated of the two, fitted better into what was expected of them, and this Virginia envied. She herself seemed to have no such role to play, and in consequence felt excluded and angry. Refusing to be relegated to the limbo of the misunderstood and neglected, she protested, feeling herself torn between resentment and admiration of her sister. On her side Vanessa was conscious that the situation was no fault of hers – and withstood the attacks in silence and with dignity, even when Virginia's tongue, with unerring intelligence, struck at her most vulnerable parts.

There was another source of envy, very natural in sisters so close to each other with one adored brother between them. As the two eldest, Thoby and Vanessa had been as thick as thieves, until Virginia, enlightened by her sense of inferiority and unfairness, realised how entrancing their relationship was and, jealous of both, insinuated herself into Thoby's affections. He, a manly schoolboy and budding intellectual, probably taught both sisters much in different ways, though one would judge – merely from looking at his photograph – that he was secretive and inhibited. Vanessa probably enjoyed his nascent masculinity and gave him in return her motherly advice and protection, while with Virginia he discussed ideas and literature. Though apparently unconcerned, Vanessa now found herself for the first time a victim of sisterly competition.

Vanessa was fifteen when her mother died, after some weeks of illness – she was forty-nine. She looked far older, worn out not only by a life of service to others but also, one is tempted to think looking at the later photographs, from an indefinable inner anguish. When two years later, after a few months of marriage, Stella died, the family was doubly bereft, while the display of extreme emotion indulged in by Leslie brought his children together in a common dislike of hypocrisy. It was now that Vanessa was forced to shoulder the burden of Virginia's early breakdowns when, even though other friends were concerned, it was to Vanessa that Virginia looked first and foremost for support and encouragement. For many years Vanessa wrote to Virginia every day of her life, and though no doubt we miss many of the overtones of a spirit that was predominantly ironic, the prevailing mood was one of tactful concern. Virginia learnt to rely on a constant sense of sympathy, while Vanessa miraculously maintained an affectionate humour without which Virginia would never have listened to her. Vanessa came to symbolise, even more than she had always done, reassurance and stability; Virginia clung to her with the desperation of one who feels threatened. It was an attitude which caught at Vanessa's most vulnerable point, and confirmed a relation which in time became something of a stranglehold.

Virginia's feelings for Vanessa were two-fold: love, admiration and understanding played their part but were inextricably mixed with jealousy and envy, stimulated by Vanessa's cool detachment and evident if unconscious superiority. With the years Virginia built up a fictional personality for Vanessa, in an effort to reduce those characteristics she found too disturbing, while emphasising others which to Vanessa herself seemed absurdly irrelevant. In a letter written many years later, Vanessa says, 'I explained how Virginia since early youth has made it her business to create a character for me according to her own wishes and has now so succeeded in imposing it upon the world that the preposterous stories are supposed to be true because so characteristic . . .' Although Vanessa talks of this character, she does not substantiate or describe it. But it was a bogey to her, one which she felt powerless to counteract. Virginia herself admits to creating the image in this letter to Duncan Grant of 1917: '. . . indeed one of the concealed worms of my life has been a sister's jealousy – *of* a sister I mean; and to feed this I have invented such a myth about her that I scarce know one from t'other.'

It was not only the falsity of this character, so brilliantly and ruthlessly improvised by Virginia for her own ends, that Vanessa found inadmissible. She half-suspected her friends of finding it more amusing and attractive than the real thing, and could not dismiss the possibility that they might be right – indeed there were moments when she felt that she herself hardly knew what the real thing was. She found herself in a position of hopeless resistance because Virginia's need to destroy – albeit by an act of creation – was stronger than her own means of self-protection: she was, to all intents and purposes, paralysed. Jockeyed by Virginia into the role of eternal mother, oracle and protector, she felt extraordinarily ill at ease, as though put into a strait-jacket. Although she had helped to cut it out herself, it was a garment that soon ceased to fit and that she longed to forget: it was difficult to forgive a sister who, she felt, should have been more perceptive, and more considerate. Thus Virginia's egotism and Vanessa's passivity contributed towards a situation that was, like some illnesses, chronic.

For reasons that resembled Virginia's sense of abandonment, but with a deeper reluctance to surrender to them, Vanessa was self-reliant almost to a fault, producing an effect of rocklike stability that was not as secure as it seemed. For the rest of her life she spent a large part of her energy in creating and maintaining a circle of safety, within which she could gather together all the elements she most loved and depended on. Her mother's early death may well have stimulated a fear of the outside world and a deep need of family life. It probably made her wary of contracting relationships further afield, and her first love affair, almost certainly unconsummated, was with her brother-in-law Jack Hills, recently widowed by the death of Stella. At the time, marriage between brother and sister-in-law was prohibited, and although it could have been legally sanctioned abroad, the attraction was not strong enough to withstand the disapproval of Stella's relatives, including her elder brother George. It died a natural death, and Vanessa waited a further seven years before allowing herself to be tempted into marriage.

Although Vanessa was unequivocally feminine, she was never the kind of woman around whom men cluster. There was an elemental quality in her sexuality by which men were either seduced or alarmed. She refused to capitulate to the values of the social set to which her half-brother George tried to introduce her. Most of the women there either hid their sexual aspirations behind a barrier of puritanism, which seemed to Vanessa purely hypocritical, or openly traded them for material and social advantages. Unworldly and lacking in social *savoir faire*, she found herself in opposition to both sexes. Full of unspoken criticism, she was disinclined to spend her energy on small talk and gave the impression of being unapproachable, an impression reinforced by the rather withdrawn expression on her face. Among those with whom she had little in common this attitude formed a barrier, threatening to turn her into that puzzling thing, a lovely woman who does not want to be attractive. When George insisted on taking her out to dinner parties, she remained aware that none of his friends would ever make a husband for her – not even Joseph Chamberlain, with whom to her relief she was able to carry on an after-dinner conversation about butterflies.

Meanwhile she profited from and greatly enjoyed her years as a student at the Academy Schools, which confirmed her sense of vocation as a painter, providing her at the same time with a refuge from a home dominated by a frail and elderly father, whose behaviour, sometimes painfully ridiculous, became less and less easy to put up with. In 1904, after a long illness, he died, and the younger part of the family removed to Bloomsbury.

Here at last, having spent most of her life immersed in a literary atmosphere, Vanessa felt free to express herself. Her easel painting already showed the sense of equilibrium which remained one of her most personal qualities, while for the first time interior decoration became a practical possibility. At last the restrictions of convention could be swept aside and her mind and heart concentrated on painting. To see her in later life, brush in hand, was to see her happy, and to think of her without her painting

24

would be to take away half her reason for living. No other activity or relationship gave her quite that kind of happiness: with children or lovers there was always an element of anxiety whereas while she was painting, though difficulties seemed insuperable, she could afford to forget herself and attain a degree of absorption which made her feel immune to anguish.

With Thoby at Cambridge Vanessa came to know a number of his friends, among them Clive Bell. Vivacious, amusing and somewhat of a libertine, Clive came from a family of *nouveaux riches* whose extreme conventionality had driven him to escape first to university and then to Paris. A young man of some experience, he was overcome by just that air of mystery in Vanessa which her brother George's friends found too much for them. He fell in love while she was still living at Hyde Park Gate, but though his feelings were at first unreciprocated he persevered and, after her removal to Bloomsbury, continued to see a great deal of her.

In 1906 Vanessa, Virginia, Thoby, Clive and other friends went for a holiday to Greece, and on their return Thoby fell ill with an infection that was not immediately diagnosed. By the time the doctor had recognised it as typhoid, it was too late, and Thoby, considered by all his friends as a brilliant and promising young man, died at twenty-six – almost the same age as Stella. Two days later Vanessa accepted Clive's proposal of marriage.

No doubt Vanessa had turned to Clive as one of her brother's most intimate friends. Her need of him may well have been impelled by the same need of identification that led to her falling in love with Jack Hills on the death of Stella. But whether this was true or not, she and Clive shared the same sense of shock, and the mutual attraction that accompanied it was natural enough – an attraction that had after all been simmering for some time.

Initially their union was a great success. She was twenty-eight and had waited a long time for sexual experience. Now that it had come, she was transfigured; she was bowled over not only by sex itself but by the intimacy it conferred on their relationship. All her tender, delicate and most endearing qualities came to the surface;

she teased, joked and laughed, enjoying the half-private, half-public parade of their feelings for each other. In addition, she soon found she was pregnant: in 1908 her elder son Julian was born.

It was during this supremely happy and fulfilled period that Virginia took it into her head to flirt with Clive, an act which paralleled in its incestuous nature that of Vanessa falling in love with Jack Hills. But its character was entirely different. Vanessa's feelings had, one may imagine, been prompted by despair at losing her sister and a desire to identify with her through the loved one by means of sexual attraction, whereas Virginia's feelings for Clive were barely sexual, and owed much of their vivacity to a common delight in the processes of the intellect. Both he and she were carried away by a youthful effervescence which ignited a whole train of intellectual fireworks in a style that was not in Vanessa's nature. Clive's manner, though flattering and suggestive, carried with it none of the undertones of feeling which would have frightened Virginia, but was exactly calculated to promote a flirtation which, as they must both have been aware, was outrageous in its apparent disregard of Vanessa's existence.

It seems as though neither Virginia nor Clive were the first to embark upon this relationship. My own interpretation is that it happened largely because, unable to share Vanessa's absorption in her very young baby, they both felt unhappy and excluded, and were thrown together. Perhaps Virginia, still in an unstable condition more than a year after the death of Thoby, allowed herself to be tempted into a potentially dangerous situation, forgetting that Clive was a man of flesh and blood, all too human in his responses to woman. More than his equal intellectually, she did not bargain for physical attraction, yet Clive's evident admiration went to her head.

It is also possible that when Vanessa had originally broken the news of her engagement, she had been too happy to be tactful and was inconsiderate of Virginia's susceptibilities, thus leaving in Virginia's mind the impression of a forceful personality that would stop at nothing to get what it wanted; so that from the beginning Virginia had suffered from a feeling of exclusion. Later intensified by Vanessa's preoccupation with her baby, this feeling became shared by Clive who, finding his sister-in-law within easy range, was unable to resist the appeal of her beauty, let alone her intelligence.

It was not, however, Clive's attention that Virginia wanted to attract, but Vanessa's: her behaviour constituted an appeal for help addressed to Vanessa over Clive's body. Nor was it simply an appeal for inclusion in her sister's married life, but a protest against being asked to stand on her own and forgo Vanessa's vigilant protection. Thoby symbolised virginity and the almost irresponsible games of adolescence at which Virginia was an adept. Now that he had disappeared she was not only faced with an intolerable loss, but was also being asked to share in the happiness of a physical maturity with which she felt unable to sympathise, and certainly did not experience with Clive. Such a demand made her feel painfully inadequate, and appeared quite unacceptable. She retaliated with another, that Vanessa should give up her husband. Its complete lack of common sense indicates the depth of her anguish: she leaped to the conclusion that she had lost Vanessa's love for ever. Virginia never wanted Clive for his own sake, and it must have been Vanessa's awareness of this that led to her restraint, not least with Clive, against whom she seems to have harboured no resentment.

One imagines that a quiet word or two would have put an end to the whole thing. Why didn't Vanessa, who was in an unassail-able position, utter them? Apart from her innate dislike of emotional confrontation, her silence may have hidden a nascent doubt about her feelings for Clive – feelings which cannot have been improved by his behaviour – and at the same time a reluctance to tell Virginia that she was tired of looking after her, a reluctance justified by Virginia's lack of stability.

So the flirtation, never consummated, came to no definite conclusion: it revived, off and on, from 1908 until 1914. I feel my brother Quentin is right when, in his biography of Virginia, he says: 'On the whole the break-up of the Bell marriage, that is to say its transformation into a union of friendship, which was slowly accomplished during the years 1911–14, made for a relaxation of tension between the sisters and a slow dissolution (never quite complete) of Virginia's long troubled relationship with Clive.' Although Virginia never obtained any deep physical or spiritual satisfaction from it, it was too stimulating and too flattering to be given up.

Whatever the truth, Vanessa's trust had, however, been shaken: Virginia not only wanted more than was reasonable to ask, but had betrayed their former relationship. It was an episode that left behind a permanent scar. Years later, seeing them together, in spite of their habitual ironic affection and without any idea of the cause, I could see in their behaviour a wariness on the part of Vanessa, and on Virginia's side a desperate plea for forgiveness. This attitude had not arisen out of the blue; it was evidence of an incident which, though long past, could not be forgiven because it had not been fully acknowledged. Both sisters had frozen into attitudes which they found painful and which prevented the normal flow of feeling.

With the birth of her sons Julian in 1908, and Quentin in 1910, Vanessa's second passion in life, maternity, was fulfilled. At Asheham, the house in Sussex taken by Virginia and shared with Vanessa, she effortlessly organised a life where friends, children and animals lived together in acceptable though primitive conditions. Surrounded by other painters, and visited by a shifting population of guests, among whom were Roger Fry and Duncan Grant, she enjoyed working in their company while controlling their existence with gentle laissez-faire. Her sense of humour, her flair for improvisation and her sympathy for other people's emotional difficulties, together with her unquestionable capacity to get what she wanted, gave her a special place among that group of friends who were later to be called Bloomsbury. They recognised in her a force that was more full-blooded and more intransigent than their own, an emotional power that had to be reckoned with, even though it was seldom expressed directly. If Vanessa adopted them with all the strength of her nature as a sort of extended family, she required from them an allegiance, almost an obedience, which they seemed to give willingly, feeling that her combination of beauty and maternal authority was almost irresistible. Most of these friends were young men, many of them, though not by any means all, homosexual. Vanessa, though a sympathetic friend and listener, did not take their love affairs very seriously: sexual emancipation, though a source of some trouble and a good deal of amusement, was hardly as important as friendship.

Vanessa's prejudices went deep and could be formidable, but their nature was personal and idiosyncratic. When they were not aroused, her tolerance, both moral and ideological, was almost unlimited. This fact, together with her sense of humour, played an important part in her relations with the opposite sex, who were both disarmed and reassured by her ability to defuse intensity and see the funny side of things. Her humour was anything but noisy and abrasive; neither was it, like Virginia's, brilliant and high-spirited. It had its moments of inspiration, however, which seemed to owe their soft explosions to some profundity of which she herself was largely unaware. Without invention or fantasy her jokes were comments, depending for some of their quality on a dry common sense that to her seemed obvious enough – and to others was a source of amazement and joy. She often misquoted a proverb, or put two together to produce a mixture that to other ears was both bizarre and delightful, such as 'It's a long worm that has no turning,' or 'It's an ill wind that makes the leopard change his spots.' Her habitual form of expression, one might even say her frame of mind, was ironic. In spite of the sense of power that emanated from her she was seldom direct, seldom sustained; when on occasion she saw things in black and white, a single word or phrase was enough to show where her feelings lay, escaping from her almost against her will. Usually, however, her meaning was too subtle to be appreciated without seeing her smile, which qualified everything she

Vanessa at Charleston, 1929

said. She seemed to appreciate a subject from both sides at once, and, unable to choose between them would laugh deprecatingly at herself, mischievously at others. Although inevitably she sometimes wounded, her irony arose from her affection and aimed at making others laugh at themselves. It was also a means of showing her love, particularly at moments when excessive seriousness seemed to be the only alternative.

With intimate friends she seemed to ride the waves like a ship at anchor, but if from any quarter she felt menace in the air, she reacted strongly with an invincible mixture of prejudice and logic. It was when using both of these together that she was most ruthless, as well as most unanswerable. Such moods were rare, though most of her friends caught glimpses of them. She was extraordinarily self-controlled and, quite often simply bored by human preoccupations, she would return to her own world, just as compelling to her as that of her children.

It was this side of her nature which hurt and eventually cooled the ardour of Roger Fry, who fell passionately in love with her in 1910–11. After Quentin's birth in August 1910, the relationship between Clive and Vanessa seems to have deteriorated. He had never ceased to have extra-marital relations and when Quentin's refusal to put on weight was causing Vanessa considerable anxiety, Clive offered her little support. It was then that Roger Fry, whom she had known for some time, showed a sympathetic understanding which, coming from a man, was new to her. Their friendship, already stimulated by a common excitement about the latest developments in art and his inauguration of the first Post-Impressionist Show in November of the same year, grew steadily more intimate. In 1911, together with Clive, they went to Turkey, where Vanessa became seriously ill. While Clive absented himself as much as possible from the sick-room, Roger revealed himself an expert, if unconventional nurse. On Vanessa's recovery and their return to London, it was evident, at least to themselves, that they were very much in love.

It must have seemed to Vanessa as though she had found the ideal partner. Although heterosexual, Roger had a feminine dimension that prevented him from being either indifferent or a bully. He showed a capacity for enthusiasm which swept aside Vanessa's hesitations. She was both amazed and amused by the unselfconsciousness with which he engaged in any new relationship or activity, and was touched by his effort to understand her feelings. Moreover, while he showed unlimited sympathy for the new art, his prestige as an expert introduced her to a part of the art world previously unknown to her, and allowed her to see pictures by old masters that would otherwise have remained inaccessible; as Roger talked of them she realised that his appreciation gained a special insight from the fact that he was a painter himself.

At the same time, Vanessa was a prey to intermittent but crippling bouts of lethargy lasting over a couple of years, suggesting that she suffered from a severe depression, different in effect but not perhaps unrelated to Virginia's instability. Whatever their cause, these periods of forced inactivity and withdrawal certainly coloured her attitude to her love affair, which had begun with her as the victim and Roger as the knight errant, rescuing her from the dangers of inertia and despair; later, when she discovered that his very vitality exhausted her and that he demanded an attention she could not give, he became a prey to self-pity while she felt a growing indifference.

For a long time he continued to be in love while she, her interest already engaged elsewhere, attempted both to assuage his longing for her while denying him any real satisfaction. In the end Roger understood that perseverance was useless, and gave up his place in her affections to another artist and friend of both, Duncan Grant. The spirit in which Roger watched the development of this new relationship, though not without moments of jealousy, was remarkable for its generosity. With Roger, Vanessa had found too much excitement, sympathy and tenderness to cut him out of her life entirely; neither of them wanted such a thing – the sacrifice would have been disproportionate, and they had too much in common for it to be possible. For the rest of his life there remained between them the flavour of a past love affair, as though neither of them would ever quite admit that it was over.

Vanessa clung to Roger, Duncan, myself and Julian, and perhaps to a lesser degree Quentin – who had his own system of
self-protection – like a limpet. An apparently strong, even self-
sufficient character, when it came to love, she bent like a flower
under the weight of a humble bee. It was her way of loving,
actuated by as great a need to be loved as to love. When the
moment came to separate, either from children or lover, in spite
of all her good intentions, she was unable to recognise it; the
stream of desire continued to be transmitted – like the messages
of animals and insects – irresistibly. When someone she loved
died, she was so disorientated that she fastened onto the nearest
person who seemed to offer both safety and an echo of the one
lost. Even when she ceased to be 'in love', she needed evidence of
her power over the loved one. Clive and Roger both hovered
nearby, compelled by her need, as later did Duncan. Luckily all
were, in their different ways, equal to saving their skins.

Duncan Grant was a cousin of the Stracheys, whom Vanessa had
known well all her life. His world was therefore much closer to
hers than either Clive's or Roger's, although, like that of the
Stracheys, it had a strong Anglo-Indian flavour. Duncan's father
had spent his professional life in India, and Duncan lived with his
parents there and in Burma until he was seven. His parents
staying on, he then lived with the Stracheys, and went to various
schools in England, where he shone with a fitful brightness
almost entirely dependent on whether or not the art master was
equal to his job. Like Vanessa, Duncan decided early in life that
all he wanted to do was to paint, an ambition encouraged by his
grandmother, Lady Strachey. He went to Paris for a year, from
where he returned to enter the London art scene. He was a
homosexual with bisexual leanings, though at what age he
realised this is not clear – perhaps he had always known it. On the
surface he seemed singularly candid and uncomplicated, with an
unselfconscious charm that had an almost hypnotic effect on
those who knew him. It was his capacity to forget himself and to

Duncan, *c.* 1916

34

remain the same under almost any circumstances, allied to an instinctive acceptance of the other person, which won for him the affection of all kinds of people. They realised that here was that very rare thing, a man almost without preconceptions, someone who has not made up his mind beforehand what to think. He was profoundly convinced that every living creature, even a mouse or an insect, had a right to its own point of view.

He was a sympathetic companion, beautiful rather than handsome and extraordinarily sensitive to the prevailing atmosphere. Albeit a cousin of the Stracheys, he was neither highly educated nor literary, in Vanessa's understanding of the term, and in consequence she did not find him threatening. In his presence, even more than in that of the intellectual Roger, Vanessa could feel at ease. Neither did she have the reservations about Duncan's painting that she had about Roger's, which created – and continued to create – a barrier between them. With Duncan she knew that the slightest allusion to aesthetics or the process of painting would be understood and appreciated, while at the same time she need not be over-serious. In addition, Duncan's emotional demands appeared easy to satisfy. Merely observing him, laughing at their friends and working together seemed to Vanessa sufficient happiness.

None the less, had it been possible to lead a normal social life, their relationship might not have continued. But it was wartime and Duncan, as a conscientious objector, was forced to live in the country and work on the land. No one better than Vanessa could have given him the moral support he needed. First at Wissett in Suffolk and then at Charleston, they succeeded in creating a life that seemed like an idyll snatched from the horror that surrounded them, and Vanessa found herself a role which exactly suited her, that of mother-housekeeper and presiding genius as well as artist. Lack of food, comfort and intelligent servants was not enough to destroy their optimism, to which the existence of two lively boys added its own special quality. For Vanessa, now about thirty-eight, association with someone six years younger than herself must have brought with it a feeling of renewal, although in time it became clear that Duncan felt she was asking for something he could not give.

Both in the house at Suffolk and afterwards at Charleston, Vanessa found she had to share Duncan with David Garnett who, younger even than Duncan, had allowed himself to be seduced. Duncan was very much in love, and Vanessa saw that if she was to keep Duncan in her life she would have to accept not only David but many others. One might imagine that such a situation would be difficult if not painful for all three – and perhaps it was. But Vanessa knew exactly what she wanted. She persuaded Duncan to give her a child, prepared to take the responsibility on herself provided he remained close to her. For her he was a genius, his offspring destined to be exceptional.

2

A Child at Charleston

I was born on December 25th, 1918, a date which to Vanessa seemed auspicious, and which, later, she taught me to associate with the unusual, as though the accident of being born on Christmas Day was a virtue of my own. Whether her feelings owed their origin to the fact that it was the first Christmas after the war, the first Christmas of peace, or just because it was a festival which still possessed a certain magic even for unbelievers, I don't know. Or was it that, my origins being unsanctioned by marriage, I was thought to need good luck, or even that, as the child of a union she considered remarkable, I shone with a special aura?

Presumably it was with his approval that Vanessa and Clive decided to ignore the fact that Duncan was my father. It was arranged between them that Duncan, on my arrival in this world, was to telegraph Clive's parents, Mr and Mrs Bell, in Clive's name. They, innocent and conventional, would never suspect, it was supposed, that I was not their grandchild. Clive was anxious to avoid the inexplicable which was not so much that his wife had been unfaithful to him – and he to her – but that this made little difference to the amity of their relations.

Clive and Vanessa must have made the decision together in a spirit that, lightheartedly, they imagined unconventional – for that is the way it was later presented to me. But parents and parents-in-law have always been misled about such things: given the freedom that Bloomsbury supposed it had won for itself, it is, on the contrary, the conventionality of the deception that is surprising. It was characteristic, however, of Clive's urbanity and Vanessa's tact: if it was unnecessary to say anything, why say it? No doubt she had other reasons, which probably had more to do with Duncan than with Clive or his family. For Vanessa, Duncan was almost an adolescent – if one reads the letters he wrote to her at this time, such an assessment seems justified. When, many years later, she came to tell me of my parentage, she offered Duncan's youth as an excuse for his behaviour, the only sign as far as I remember that she was aware of anything wrong. He was at that time thirty-three or thirty-four. She thought of him as, above all, an artist; to see him as a father seemed unreal, and perhaps unnecessary, since she herself felt equal to being both father and mother. Duncan's own feelings are unknown to me.

Not only did Clive's parents have to be taken into account, but also Duncan's – or so I assume. Major Grant would probably have thought that something should be done, even that Duncan should marry Vanessa, which none of them wanted. Everything was all right as it was; they did not want the older generation meddling in what was primarily a practical situation already settled to their own satisfaction. As far as intimate friends were concerned, my birth was an open secret: the only voice of criticism was that of Bunny Garnett, who told Vanessa that in depriving me of my true father she was making a rash decision. Clive, more detached than Vanessa and wiser than Duncan, may have foreseen certain difficulties: he himself had to put up with what must at the time have been an embarrassing situation, though no one seemed to consider it as such. Owing to my likeness to Duncan, even my grandmother Ethel must soon have had her suspicions. I was the only person successfully kept in the dark.

Charleston, the house where I was born, was a large, compact Sussex farmhouse, standing by itself just under Firle Beacon, the highest point in the range of downs that extends from the River Cuck in the east to the Ouse in the west. At the foot of the Beacon was a cornfield, and between this field and the house lay the farm buildings, dominated by a magnificent flint barn and granary, underneath which stood the hay-wagons and tumbrils, at the time still in use. They were drawn across the chalk roads by huge brown horses, while the red-and-white cows munched their fill in the fields and the rickyard was full of haystacks, bristly and compact. In front of the house was a pond, beyond that an orchard, and lying next to it on the north side was a large walled garden.

The property never belonged to my family; my mother rented it from the farmer, who himself had it on a lease from the owner, Lord Gage. Vanessa was not interested in owning property, preferring the feeling that she could at any time change her mind and go somewhere else. She discovered Charleston in 1916, just when she needed a refuge for herself and her two sons, and for Duncan and Bunny. As conscientious objectors, Duncan and Bunny worked on Mr Hex's farm a few miles away, returning at teatime, happy to find themselves in the sympathetic atmosphere created by Vanessa. Friends came for the week-end, and a close relationship was maintained not only with those who came from London, such as Maynard Keynes, Roger Fry and Lytton Strachey, but with Leonard and Virginia, who, until they moved to Rodmell, were often at Asheham, only four miles away.

With the arrival of peace, however, the *ménage à trois* was to split up; though Duncan and Bunny were both there when I was born, they were longing to get back to a semblance of normal life in London after the rigours and isolation of the war, and Bunny, whose tastes had been only temporarily homosexual, was already attracted by the idea of other and quite different love affairs. It was only Vanessa who was immobilised – worried by a domestic crisis and almost certainly by the fear that Duncan might finally desert her, in spite of the fact that he was now the father of her child.

In addition, almost immediately after my birth I fell ill, an illness reluctantly admitted by the local doctor, who did not know what remedy to prescribe. Vanessa, very worried, sent a message to her friend Noel Olivier, who, unable to come herself, persuaded a Dr Moralt to make her way down to Charleston. Responding to her treatment, I began to thrive on Gray's Powders and cow's milk. My two brothers, Julian and Quentin, ten and eight years older than myself, showed their feelings at my arrival in the world by running amok in the schoolroom, and were sent to stay with Virginia, while Vanessa lay in bed in a house without running water, electricity or telephone. True, the war was over, but food and coal were still scarce, and in addition to her anxiety on my account, Vanessa had difficulty in finding servants. Five years later, writing to Margery Snowden, a friend she had met twenty years earlier at the Academy Schools, Vanessa described the situation thus:

Charleston   *Christmas 1923*
. . . Here we are spending a very domestic Christmas. Really I think I shall advertise it. 'Mr and Mrs Clive Bell and family at home at Charleston, Christmas 1923 – no one else admitted.'. . . I haven't been here at this time since five years ago when Angelica was born. It was very romantic then – the first Christmas of peace and a most lovely moonlit, frosty night. I remember waking up in the early morning after she had been born and hearing the farm-men come up to work singing carols and realising it was Christmas Day, and it seemed rather extraordinary to have a baby then – perhaps I seem very sentimental, do I? but the horrors afterwards, when she nearly died through the doctor's idiocy and every possible domestic disaster seemed to happen together, were so great that I rather forgot the happy part of it. I don't think I've ever had such an awful time. But those sort of horrors are unreal in a sense – except the anxiety – they go and leave nothing. I daresay I'm becoming too reminiscent – you see the consequences of being in the same place again after five years.

My first conscious memory is not of Charleston but of France, always to me a second home, and of being carried, probably by Vanessa, up a flight of dark stairs, to find at the top a small, voluble lady in black, who gave me violet *bon-bons*. We were in Paris and she was almost certainly Angela Lavelli, a friend of Roger Fry, who occasionally offered her services to Vanessa as chaperone for her children. Whether the horns of the taxis honking in the rain, typical of the voices of Paris, belong to the same occasion I don't know; and whether being put to sleep in the luggage-rack is real or only hearsay I am not sure. I seem to have felt the string of the rack, like a hammock swaying to the rhythm of the train; and when I was given soda water to drink for the first time, astonished by its autonomous activity, I christened it 'prickly water'. It was on this journey that Grace, our maid, seeing the sun reflected in the window opposite, turned to Duncan and said, in wonder, 'Are there two suns in France, Mr Grant?' It was her first visit abroad, and she thought things might be different. Julian and Quentin turned her mistake into part of the continuous myth they wove about our lives, never allowing us to forget anything that had caused them the intense, slightly malicious joys of adolescence.

We were on our way to St Tropez, where Nessa had taken La Maison Blanche, a house belonging to M. and Mme Vildrac, situated a little way outside the town. It was Christmas and my third birthday. There was a long, light-filled room, a door on to the terrace, a buzz of talk . . . I was playing with my rag doll Judy, whom I hugged passionately. I had a secret which in some mysterious way was discovered: I had a temperature and was put to bed. This was the first of many occasions when I hoped to hide an illness, dreading I hardly know what: perhaps the act of surrender that illness implied, which once accomplished can be a voluptuous pleasure. At the same time, however, it allowed all kinds of people besides Vanessa disconcerting and intimate access to my body.

I remember being in a state of great anxiety because Julian and Quentin had locked themselves in the church. I imagined them there for ever, not understanding that doors could be unlocked. I was impressed and disturbed by their audacity, since I understood that it had somehow involved an affront to the clergyman or priest. It brought home to me the difference between my brothers' lives and my own – theirs so independent, mine restrained by female authority. There I was standing in the hot dusty road with Grace and my nurse Nellie, in front of a white wall overtopped with black cyprus, waiting for someone to fetch the key. The sunbaked landscape reflected the heat of midday, the hour when everything begins to tremble and the smell of southern cooking invades the air.

Another memory is one of extreme pleasure tinged with disbelief. Held in someone's arms, I looked from a height into the shallow transparencies of a square pool contained within a band of grey granite. (I always supposed it was a municipal pool on the *Place* at St Tropez, but when I looked for it some years later it was not to be seen.) In a corner floated a couple of chinchilla cushions encircled by brown fringes, their centres blotched with blobs of rich brown, dark blue and white. It may have been the sight of these creatures that gave rise to my nickname, Jellyfish or Jellycat.

A fourth memory is of a dream, which still gives me a feeling of pleasure, perhaps because it was in the tempera colours of Fra Angelico. In it Nellie and I walked along a beach which was entirely made of those tiny, fragile pink shells one finds on occasion by the sea. These I collected in a little box, while we slowly advanced beside the shining waves of ultramarine towards a tall cupboard, standing against the sky, ready to hold my treasure. The cupboard, painted with a design of yellow discs, is still standing in Vanessa's old bedroom at Charleston.

It is at Charleston that I am next aware of myself. In photographs of the time I am grave, round-eyed and healthy, held by a smiling Nellie or a Madonna-like Vanessa, whose long straight fingers are too apt to find their way into every crevice of my body. It was then, at the age of five, that I first became aware of my own identity, and with it of an exaggerated sweetness in Vanessa which troubled me. Alongside the everyday brown-bread-and-butter of my life in the nursery ran my relationship with her, conducted in the very different atmosphere of drawing-room and studio. My earliest sensations were of her propitiatory attitude, as though I held a weapon in my small, fat hands. Anxious not to provoke, she continually soothed and lulled me into acceptance. Cries, screams or the sight of tears upset her; if she could buy peace she was satisfied. I longed for her to want me to be strong and independent, whereas apparently all she desired was to suffocate me with caresses.

Every morning announced itself through the red and yellow curtains, which blew gently inwards over the wide floorboards. In a shaft of blue sunlight the motes of dust spiralled, dancing an invitation to the day outside. At the age of five one is nothing but a little animal: the world is made of light, colour, smells and sounds which are more urgent and compelling then than ever again. With the purity and violence of truth, life speaks its own multiple language: without need of interpretation, it is addressed intimately to oneself. I only needed time, unmeasured by the careful, restraining hand or voice, to understand all the things that shouted and whispered to me their various secrets.

The early part of the day was devoted to the walled garden. Its door opened with a rising shriek, and from the time it took to announce that it had shut, you knew, even if you couldn't see, whether more than one person had come into it. If you were there first, you could hide behind a clump of flowers or one of the upturned millstones that stood at intervals along the terrace. Sometimes, without being seen, I could get as far as the shed, filled with broken and discarded objects blanketed with spider's web. Flower-pots, still containing earth, bulbs, a dibber, a rusty trowel, a few roorkee chairs and a pile of little pieces of coloured glass, intended for making mosaics. Apart from their colour, their grainy, semi-translucent texture fascinated me: I wanted to know them, and therefore to eat them – but was prevented.

Then there was the profusion of flowers, many of which, when picked and turned upside down, could be transformed into gorgeous princesses with a dazzling change of wardrobe. Throughout the summer, many hundreds of these were abandoned, left to wilt in a corner of the garden.

The garden walls were of flint and brick, supported here and there by sloping brick buttresses. Inside it was warm and sheltered, alive with the noises of insects and birds, which sounded different from those outside. In the early morning the sun shone through a milky mist, fragmented into particles of blue and scarlet. As it vanished, the walls began to sing with warmth, and my attention was caught by a butterfly, black and red with blotches of white. It settled on a michaelmas daisy but, when my hand stretched out to grasp it, gently wobbled away, until the breeze lifted it up to the height of the elm that stood outside the garden wall.

In front of the house there was a patch of gravel, possibly once a perfect oval, now distorted to some other, less elegant shape. The small, uneven stones slid underfoot, but conscious of the solidity of the earth underneath, I kept my balance. Numerous tiny creatures threaded their way among the boulders: spiders, beetles, ants, busy, intent and unaware of me, a female Gulliver in their midst. Giant though I was, I was perhaps less aware than they of our difference in scale. I was each ant, each beetle; I knew what it was to have six legs and swivel eyes, to hesitate, searching for information with trembling antennae, suspicious and fearful. The long grass too was full of creatures, turning, wriggling, hopping and floating in mid-air; and the pond, what was it made of? Was it solid, deep or shallow, good to eat or drink, hot or cold? My eyes alone could not begin to answer these questions; however earnestly I looked at the water, it was always playing tricks with me. How could it be solid, brown and dirty in the corner where the yew tree stood, and on the other side reveal each tiny flint and piece of gravel, passive but quivering? To see the willow tree upside down, its grey-and-dun-coloured shape interrupted by the rippling moorhen, was to catch a glimpse of another world where everything was the other way round, the trees at the top and the clouds, racing back to front, at the bottom.

In those days the pond seemed enormous. On the side near the farm a tiny stream, coming from the downs, trickled under the road, and drained into the pond. Here the shallow water revealed a bottom of flinty shingle, over which flashed the stickleback, disappearing into beds of watercress and forget-me-not. Sometimes, peering closely, it was possible to make out a caddis worm, done up in an untidy bundle of sticks. It was here too that the cows and horses were brought to drink in the evening, sucking the water through their tremulous, sensitive lips. The cows dribbled, and stared stupidly at their reflections, but the horses, calm and intelligent, lifted their heads to see all that was going on.

On the other side of the pond, where the water was deeper, it was held in by a wall of flecked and silver flint, threaded with a line or two of brick, finished by half-round bricks. Here the water was brown, hovered over by turquoise dragonflies. The yew trees which stood on this side of the orchard, plunged their dark shadows into the confused, umber-coloured liquid which reflected nettles, grasses and trembling sky alike. Somewhere in the tangle grew a bullace tree, which yielded little scented pink plums made by Lottie the cook into delicious pies. In those days there was also a syringa or philadelphus, whose druglike perfume invaded the July evenings.

Opposite the house was a huge willow, to me the grandfather of all the trees in the garden. Its silver leaves were not only loved but approved of by Vanessa and Duncan because they were not green, a colour they condemned as ubiquitous. Beneath it quacked the fat white ducks, gently nuzzling the duckweed, which winked and sparkled in the sun, each tiny green leaf lying flat and close-packed on the surface of the water, and in summertime there was a smell of mud growing stronger with the weeks that passed. One year there was a drought, and in the centre of the cracked and fissured clay hardly more than a puddle remained. Watching the iridescent bubbles on the surface, we could see a few carp flipping in their dying agony, while the bodies of their fellows stank where they had been stranded at the edge.

Julian and Quentin spent all the morning hollowing out great lumps of chalk, transforming them into intricate castles and fortresses with galleries, towers, oubliettes and machicolations. With these they played a continuous war game, peopling them with armies of hips and haws which ran unsteadily down the grooves and hollows like ants in a heap. Too small to join in, I spent a lot of time concealed in the pampas grass which grew near the front gate, next to the bay tree in whose scented branches I had a house. When I tired of being a cook, serving up leaf-fuls of yellow-eyed daisies as poached eggs, I could follow the narrow path that ran between the pond and the long damp wall of the garden, to the orchard. Flanked by iris, it passed under the yews, where there was a carpet of dark brown needles, slippery to the feet. At the end of the path there was a Pre-Raphaelite rose that smelt of cold cream. When I was very small, Vanessa would hold me up to sniff and touch its faintly flushed petals. The grown-ups seldom came to the orchard, where twisted, unpruned apple trees, used as perches by the wood-pigeons and rooks, bore a few dozen apples that were violated first by the birds and then by the wasps. Beneath them was a tangle of bryony and lords-and-ladies, so obviously poisonous, and a mass of reedy grass long enough to close over my head, as I looked through the interstices like a tiger in the jungle.

Behind Charleston to the south lay Firle Beacon and its supporting downs, like a row of half-submerged ancient elephants. Their massive grey humps protected us from the west wind, which brought not only the rain but a sea mist which rolled down their sides and hid them from view. Sometimes I would climb up through these clouds; from above they hid the house, the farm and everything except the tops of the trees, which looked as though they protruded from a sunken forest. And then the mood would change as the downs became the mirror of the sky, and the shadows of the clouds raced across their flanks, or, at other moments, lay like a massive barrier, flat and dark against the grey hillside. Sometimes we would climb right up, disturbing myriads of silken blue butterflies flitting from one miniature flower to another, and, standing exhilarated on top of the elephant's forehead, we could see the thin pale line of the sea, and even sometimes the Channel steamer crossing from Newhaven to Dieppe. The wind, warm and gentle on a summer's day, carried with it a suspicion of salt and, blowing from the south-west, had bent the few remaining thorn trees in the same direction, like old men with a load on their backs. In those days there were still many sheep and the turf was wiry and polished. There were strange hummocks and hollows in which one could lie and look up into the blue air, until one almost fell asleep from heat and stillness, disturbed only by the zooming of a bumble-bee or the distant rattle of the electric train as it wriggled across the Weald. But it was the dew-ponds that were so strangely magical: great circles of silver lying cool and undisturbed, gazing not only at the sky but at the centuries that had passed since they were made. My nurse Louie regarded them with awe and said that a sheep or cow once fallen in could never get out again. Julian described how the clay was smoothed with infinite care, puddled with a heavy stone at the end of a staff until it became dense and waterproof like a shallow pudding basin, and how, conserving the dew, the ponds always held some liquid for parched animals.

3

Gordon Square

More than half our time was spent in London, where Vanessa was now sharing No. 46 Gordon Square with Maynard Keynes. It was a large, tall house with high rooms looking onto the square. On the first floor, french windows opened onto a balcony with a black iron railing that ran across the width of the house and was repeated all along the row. Vanessa lived in the upper part, where the rooms were much smaller and the ceilings sloped as in a country cottage. Here, in her attic sitting-room, I was handed over to her every day after tea, to play in front of the gas fire, its intricate cones of blue and white changing to red and yellow, the little bowl of dusty water placed on the hearth like an offering in front of a shrine. I sat on the chequered coconut matting, rough and uneasy to my bottom, sheltered from the heat by Nessa's knees, while her hands would take from the mantelpiece, and bring down to my level, the dried oranges and lemons she used for darning socks. I gazed at them in wonder, and threw them into the shadows. Nellie's sudden appearance at the door provoked screams of anger, and she would carry me away, scarlet and protesting, leaving behind an anguished Vanessa.

At bedtime I was sometimes allowed, as a privilege, to have my bath in Maynard's bathroom, more splendid than ours. It was a luxury chiefly because of its larger size, but there were glass jars full of sponges and bath salts, and I well remember Maynard, in his elegant city suit, standing over me and showering me with these as I sat in the water. My doll Judy was also there, her stockinette limbs splashed with red ink, which, as I carefully explained, resulted from numerous operations.

Nellie was genial, and, to judge from surviving photographs, attractive; but I never liked her, perhaps because I associated her with separation from Vanessa. She is connected too with the peculiar smell of linoleum, of a back lavatory and a dark little bedroom on the ground floor, of plates of porridge kept in the kitchen and returned to be eaten at teatime, and with a starched, unreceptive bosom. A London nightmare, which quite unjustifiably I blamed on Nellie, was a gruesome dream of white-skinned children whose arms and legs, like parsnips, were chopped off in a sea of blood. It recurred several times, and I grew to dread it.

Another London scene of that time is of Duncan standing stark naked in the back bedroom. Coming in by chance, I was amazed at the sight of him; what on earth was this strange appendage hanging between his legs? Seized by embarrassment but devoured by curiosity, I turned my back on him, bent down and, putting my head between my own legs, continued my rapt examination of his anatomy, prompted by the feeling that if I was upside down no one would spot the focus of my attention. Carried away by a smiling Vanessa, I burst into tears.

Another, quite different, occasion is also connected with Duncan. The large L-shaped room on the first floor is full of people. There are many children among the grown-ups, and in the warmth everyone is moving about and talking. There is the Christmas tree, decorated and lit with candles, and the long heavy curtains are drawn close. Standing by the sofa, I am suddenly accosted by a rather small Father Christmas. Whether he gives me anything or says anything to me I can't remember, but I am enchanted by his presence. I turn away to call attention to him, and when I turn back he has disappeared! Dismayed and disappointed, I look for him everywhere, particularly behind the curtains where it is suddenly dark, cold and frightening. Vanessa, to whom I appeal, only smiles and shakes her head; for some reason I am convinced it was Duncan – and feel horribly defrauded.

The same room saw many events, all of which were winter scenes, dark and glowing with the heat of the stove. They were moments of security, comfort and heightened enjoyment when, after tea, I had Vanessa to myself and could monopolise her. We had our favourite occupations, our favourite rituals when, even if Virginia or an intimate friend were there, Vanessa was indisputably mine. I could claim her innermost attention even while a murmur of remote talk was going on over my head. We roasted sugar lumps between the bars of the stove, turning them over so that there was a nugget of soft explosive sugar enclosed in a shell of caramel. Or I was allowed to make toast for the guests, different shades of brown for different people.

On other days we would immerse ourselves in the intricacies of paper-cutting: Vanessa would gently soothe my annoyance at my own clumsiness, performing miracles with her long, be-ringed fingers. She would concentrate, frowning, the light from the stove glinting on her spectacles, while I watched a shape slowly forming under the slicing of the scissors, finally resolving itself into a row of ballet dancers that could actually stand on the table. One year saw a craze for exotic flowers which nodded and dangled at the end of long canes. Virginia was a good client for such products and often went home with her hands full. I remember one painting lesson, almost the only one Vanessa ever gave me, when she drew a little dog and surrounded him with a sea of black, giving him at the same time some pale green shadows. This, she said, was the secret of making him as white as snow.

In the far-away basement Mrs Harland, Maynard's cook, presided over the shining kitchen range. Tiny and vivacious, she had the skin of a wild rose, and seemed always to be making pastry. Rows of jam tarts covered the well-scrubbed kitchen table, their jewelled centres suggesting fragments of stained glass or the rings on Nessa's dressing-table. I was often given a lick of jam or a piece of cake to celebrate my visits to that subterranean region where her husband, Pa Harland, was to be seen cleaning the silver in a small room with a baize door, called the pantry. He was said by the grown-ups to be lazy and untrustworthy, and he smelled strongly of whisky – but his Cockney charm had captivated Maynard, and continued to do so for some years. He always welcomed me with warmth, and I would consent, when there was a party, to being carried upstairs on his shoulders –

from where the smell of whisky almost overcame me – to find myself in the drawing-room on the first floor full of powdered and scented ladies in parakeet-coloured chiffon; holding glasses in their hands and smoking cigarettes, they all seemed to be in a state of great excitement. Out of sight behind the door, Pa Harland would feed me on left-over strawberries and cream.

London was filled with high dark buildings and hard surfaces, stone pavements and iron railings, areas filled with dustbins and steamy kitchen windows, and in the square huge plane trees with spotted, sooty trunks. In winter fog lurked in the air, and when it descended, a proper pea-souper, it entered the house by every crevice and enveloped the world in obnoxious but exciting unreality. The sound of the descending silence was ominous; the leaves dropped from the trees with noiseless finality to lie inert on the paths and pavement. The lights of a car would loom uncertainly from the limbo of the street, and if we were out we would hurry home, our throats and noses choked with smog. Indoors the gas fire seemed like an island, or far-off lighthouse, and we would sit there gazing at it and munching our buttered crumpets.

Opposite the house was the square, encircled by the ubiquitous iron railings, enclosing a little world of paths and lawns, privet bushes and plane trees, and an ancient weeping ash which hung over a circular wooden seat. This was my playground, one in which I have no memory of meeting other children, but where I was perfectly happy if left to myself, lost in my imagination, but alive, as dogs and cats are, to the pungent smells of soot, privet, wet earth and grass that surrounded me. It was good to be allowed out even into such a limited arena, and there were moments when I felt impelled to push my nose between the railings to get an idea of what was going on outside. Everyone seemed extraordinarily busy – they mostly hurried past, looking neither to right nor left, concentrated on some personal problem. I stared unmoved, mystified by the behaviour of what seemed to be a distantly related species.

The square was also a meeting ground where, if I had not already been hustled off to bed, I would sometimes see a group of familiar figures watching the tennis players and laughing at each other's jokes. In the yellow evening light the moment seemed particularly precious to them, superior to a London busy with more exciting things. Then Clive, becoming conscious of the time, would hurry off, hailing a taxi round the corner. The others would laugh, and say he was going to meet the Princess Bibesco or the wife of the French Ambassador, closing their ranks, knowing that they themselves had only a mutton chop to look forward to, without champagne. Their evening would no doubt be spent sitting under a lamp, reading anything from Tasso to the *Daily Mirror*. Conscious that all I had to look forward to was bed, the grown-ups would stare at me benignly and extend a caressing hand from time to time. It was on one such occasion that Bunny told me of the mating habits of worms, the only bit of scientific education I ever received.

On our own side of the square I knew the Keyneses, the Stracheys, my Uncle Adrian and his wife Karen Stephen, with their two daughters, Anne and Judith, whose flat was above theirs at No. 50; during the summer there were also the Bussys in the top of No. 51. Raymond Mortimer lived round one corner, and Leonard and Virginia round the other, in Tavistock Square. It was a family network that gave me the feeling that this part of London belonged to us. On fine summer evenings one could sometimes see the Stracheys on their balcony, and I was once taken to see Lady Strachey shortly before she died. She stood on the landing outside the first-floor sitting-room supporting herself with a walking stick, and looking blankly at the wall above my head, since she was almost if not quite blind. I was struck by her massive size and immobility, her white hair parted in the middle, and her black dress which came down to the ground. It may have been Marjorie Strachey who accompanied me, wanting to confront me – although I was unaware of the relationship – with my great-aunt, and to join the two extremes of youth and age, so that long afterwards I should be able to say that I had seen this formidable woman, who herself had seen George Sand at the theatre and been an intimate friend of George Eliot.

One of the rare but regular events was tea with Leonard and Virginia. Virginia I knew would treat me as a special person – almost as Vanessa did. Leonard, however, was another matter, and was the only member of the family who could successfully refuse me something I wanted, whose very tone spelt the finality of real authority, against which there was no appeal. He was dispassionate, and perhaps it was the perception of a different attitude which, while it impressed me, made me vacillate, unsure of what I wanted or why.

With the Hogarth Press in the basement and the solicitors on the ground floor I found myself in a rigorous world of machinery and accounts, very different from our own. Occasionally I collected Virginia from her writing-room in the basement, where she sat by a tiny gas fire surrounded by a wall of books done up in brown paper parcels as though to shelter her from a bombardment. I felt the austerity of their lives compared with ours – which was much fuller of wine and laughter, and of the ribaldry supplied by Julian and Quentin. Virginia and Leonard's work allowed them only just time for a frugal meal; preoccupied with thoughts of the *New Statesman* or the House of Commons, Leonard encouraged no elbows on the table, cigars or liqueurs – he was off, like a secretary-bird, to more gripping occupations. When I arrived there, I knew that my claims on his time were strictly limited. At the tea-table, where we sat in high-backed chairs as though in a nursery, Leonard pretended to talk to me like a grown-up, pinning me down by a glance from his sapphire-blue eyes, under which I shrank into being what I was – a small child. After the meal he would offer me, with ritualistic hand, a striped humbug, of which he ate one after every meal. Virginia had different sweets of her own, and I was allowed one of each.

Leonard then descended to the basement while Virginia and I retreated to the sitting-room at the top of the house, decorated by Vanessa and Duncan. It was this room which, bombed in 1940, flagrantly exhibited its coloured walls to the world at large, while the rest of the house lay collapsed into a pile of rubble. In the 1920s, however, it was an oasis of intimacy, shabby but elegant. The light shone in two yellow pools on either side of the fireplace – the scene was set for conversation. Virginia produced rolls of coloured paper which she had bought that afternoon from Kettle's in New Oxford Street, one of her favourite shops, and with scissors, paste and pins proceeded to create a doll, the image of Ottoline Morrell, over which unexpected triumph she emitted hoots of laughter. On other occasions we hung out of the front window above the parapet, throwing out lumps of sugar for the cart-horses far below, bored by waiting for their drivers. They, however, snorted with indifference, and plunged their noses into hessian bags, to munch their hay.

A year or two earlier than this Nellie went and Louie came. I accepted the change with a good grace, especially as from the first Louie possessed a moral ascendancy over me that attracted me enormously – to Vanessa this was a miracle. There were no more scenes about going to bed, and Vanessa even wondered what black arts she used – but there were none. She simply happened to be what I needed. Small and dark, she had a face like a squashed red apple with pips for eyes, and her short hair was tied up on one side by a floppy black ribbon. Timidity itself, when surprised on the stairs by Duncan or Clive she blushed all over her neck and was reduced to speechlessness – unlike Grace, who was always ready to pass the time of day, and perhaps say something foolish which was repeated with laughter at the lunch-table. In the kitchen, however, Louie could be fierce enough in favour of her own opinions. Unafraid of my tantrums, she exercised an authority based partly on affection, and partly on values inherited from generations of country people. Quite rightly, Vanessa trusted Louie and was relieved to be able to leave me in her hands; I was completely happy. Her great virtue was that she was rough and solid, and with her I learnt to a certain extent to think of things outside myself. But she was also repressed and limited, her mind like a Stilton cheese, riddled with airless little tunnels that ended in dust. She cared too much about the opinions of other people, and from her I learnt a whole string of words and phrases, a system of feeling that was utterly dull and conventional. No doubt I responded to it with relief as a change from the extreme sophistication of my family, but – although for the opposite reasons – it had the effect of stopping me from using my brains.

My brief phase of religion owed much to Louie's romanticism: she loved seeing the gentry in her Norfolk village kneeling on their embroidered hassocks, reciting the Lord's Prayer. Her morality, however, was hardly exalted, and her vision of God was very vague. He never became real to me, lacking the attraction of Jesus, who may, I now see, have seemed more like Duncan. I had one delicious dream of Him which I could not shake off for a long time – but I should imagine this had more to do with budding sexuality than with religion. After going to church with Mrs Bell at Christmas, probably in an effort to demonstrate my independence from Vanessa, I improvised a ritualistic dance for the benefit of Maynard and Lydia when they came to tea. I heard them ask Vanessa in unbelieving tones whether I was religious, to which she replied with an evasive, deprecatory remark which had an instantaneous effect, like pricking a bubble, and marked the end of my flirtation with the Lord.

4
With the Bells at Seend

At Christmas, we spent two or three days with Clive's family at Seend in Wiltshire. For me, stimulated by the celebration of both Christmas and my birthday, the visit was one of excitement and pleasure, while for Vanessa it was an annually recurring period of boredom and misery. Her dislike must have grown with time, as she felt less and less justification in being there, constantly reminded by my presence that this was neither her place, nor mine. Ignorant of both facts I was unaffected by them, but Vanessa could remember her early years there as the eldest daughter-in-law, when her visits had been unbearably long. She had no sympathy with Clive's father and found little to say to her sisters-in-law, Lorna and Dorothy, who were interested almost exclusively in horses, hounds and hunt balls. What Vanessa most disliked was the hypocrisy and pretentiousness of which the whole household was redolent, but to which I, for some years, remained insensitive. I took it all at its face value, sniffing the Victorian smells with pleasure – the leather bindings of the *Illustrated London News*, the chrysanthemums in the jardinière, the smell of the spotless earth-closet and the polish on the oak floorboards. All these, added to the formality of our existence there, the presence too of the impeccable servants (some of whom were my friends), the hierarchy of the household, meant much to me: they created a yearly dip into romance, calling to mind the books I was fond of, such as *Little Lord Fauntleroy* and *The Secret Garden*, and the novels of Charlotte M. Yonge.

From Paddington we took the train to Devizes, where we were met by Ovens, previously the coachman, now taking as much pride in his smooth purring machine with its polished ornaments, and mahogany-upholstered interior, as he had once done in plaiting tails and combing manes. Upholstered himself in navy blue velour, there he was, touching his cap and holding open the door of the car. As he covered our knees with a rug, Vanessa sank back into her seat, dumb with apprehension, whereas I was feverish with excitement. Clive sat in front and talked to Ovens with ease about local events and people, whose names he remembered effortlessly. The huge silent car navigated the roads with arrogant smoothness: I watched the silver figure on the bonnet describe an arc across the landscape as it swung round to dip between the lodge gates under the bottle-brush fir trees, some pretending they were snow-laden even when the air was muggy and the sky like a bad watercolour. The gloom of the evening was intensified by the jagged shapes of the trees, seeming to presage the long winter night. And then an arched yellow window sprang out of the blackness, and there we were, drawn up outside the pseudo-medieval porch.

No sooner had Ovens helped us out of the car than the front door swung open to reveal Grandpapa standing ready to welcome us in the glow of home-generated electricity, while the respectful figure of Ellen in cap and apron hovered to help us with our bags, unwilling to allow us to carry anything heavier than a handkerchief. The hall seemed enormous. The polished floor was dazzling, warning us of how treacherous it really was. In the bustle of our arrival Grandpapa, smelling of the Harris tweed he wore, his chin wagging under a short white beard, barked his greetings, slapping Clive on the shoulder with over-hearty goodwill. I stood there feeling trapped, fearful of what he would do. 'Put out your tongue, young lady.' I did so, with the sensations of a ravished sea anemone. 'What you need is plenty of greens to eat; three helpings of spinach a day.' Silent, I was thankful to be allowed to squirm away.

Luckily, not spinach but cake was standing on the table, spread with a white cloth which hung to the floor in Vandyke points. There were two platefuls of paper-thin cucumber sandwiches, scones and silver dishes laden with rolls of butter. Dorothy, my younger and more congenial aunt, sat placidly behind the teapot while Lorna vociferated her welcome in the raucous Bell voice;

their intimate conversation over tea resounded through the hall like toucans calling to each other in the jungle. Each had married a man destined to be a colonel: one of them was the last man off the beach at Gallipoli and the other the handsomest man in the British army. The man of courage was diffident and witty, whereas the other, though impeccably dressed and sporting a moustache, was the greatest bore in the county. Grandmamma, small and soft, kissed us and murmured her conventional greetings, while Vanessa and I, glad of our tea, sat down to answer all the customary questions about our lives during the past year. The men took their cups and stood a little apart, sipping through their moustaches and talking about local events and the weather, as though these were hardly fit subjects for women.

The hall was the centre of the house. A gallery ran round two sides, and off these were the bedrooms, whose privacy was maintained behind doors of solid oak. Opposite were mullioned windows, their deep window seats suggesting the Jacobean age. At one end, high up, hung the head of a moose shot by Grandpapa, the date and place of its death inscribed on a brass plaque immediately below it. At the other end of the hall was a glass case enlivened with a backcloth of Highland rocks and a greenish sky framing a stuffed heron, several grebe pecking in real sand, and, beside them, a frond or two of sympathetic grass. The whole house was hung with guns and pistols, swords and daggers, arranged fan-wise, suggesting a life of fantasy that in retrospect makes Grandpapa seem more interesting. Did he dream, as in the Civil War, of being besieged? Or was it simply ostentation, like most of his other activities? Obviously he had his fantasies, however little he was willing to admit their existence, but they suggested nothing good or attractive: everywhere were the symbols of the destroyer or the poor, dead and stuffed destroyed. Every corner held antlers of various sizes; paws, tails, mangy heads looked down from the walls in glassy impassivity, while in the mahogany cases there were stuffed squirrels, or once-charming, elusive waterfowl. Outside Vanessa's bedroom lay a snarling tiger, his scalloped length etched in blood-red felt.

The house was a kind of petrified zoo. In the library a lamp stood on a tripod of hooves, once those of a deer, and on the writing-table, furnished with the thickest of inlaid writing-papers, was an ink-well made from another, larger hoof, perhaps that of the moose in the hall, king of all these relics. In the dining-room, pepper and salt were shaken out of a pair of silver owls, not of course stuffed and for that very reason more attractive. Every feather on their backs was etched with care, and they stood proud and steady on their metal feet. Most of the pictures were of animals – hounds, horses, dogs, including a large, unctuous chow, one of the dynasty which reigned over the life of Grandmamma. Lorna and Dorothy were not painted in evening-dress but on the back of a favourite hunter, as was Grandpapa in a pink coat as Master of Hounds. Vanessa, having been asked to revive its appearance, covered this picture with varnish which came up in bubbles – surely a Freudian demonstration. Fond though the Bells were of animals, I doubt if they understood them more than most people. They looked to them for support, needing their loving if mute approbation.

On Christmas Eve we decorated the hall. Julian and Quentin with their cousin Thomas climbed up to the moose, while his sister Barbara and I were permitted to put ivy round the bookcases. Finally all was pronounced splendid, and we sometimes had time for a game of puff-billiards in the drawing-room where Grandmamma had remained sitting in front of the fire. Although on her account we tried to control our hysteria, it usually attracted a grown-up or two, who stood behind us almost as convulsed as we ourselves were until the dressing-bell sounded, when we went upstairs to change for dinner. One of my delights at Seend were the bathrooms, tucked away into corners of the house and lined with deep-green Doulton tiles. The large bath was encased in mahogany, its brass taps jutting generously over the edge to gush with soft brown water. The earth-closet next door smelled of cinders and Jeyes fluid; its wooden seat extended from wall to wall, with a cover which one removed entirely before sitting over the hole. A little recess at the side contained paper and a shovel, so that one could cover one's excrement with ashes like a cat, a most satisfactory proceeding. After the bath, still damp and lobster-coloured, attired in my party dress, I would dash to Vanessa's room to show myself for her approval before descending to the dining-room at the sound of the second bell.

The gentlemen wore smoking jackets, the ladies low necks, and bits of jewellery and long skirts. Vanessa, the only beautiful woman present, put on her garnet earrings, which swung from her ears like bunches of grapes with golden leaves. Her dresses were often home-made and embroidered with unorthodox designs in large stitches which looked splendid but unusual when seen beside the odd bits of lace and chiffon worn by the others. Her manner, at variance with her appearance, was hesitant and conciliatory as well as a trifle frigid, betraying to those who knew her well her inner anguish and boredom.

After Grandpapa's death in 1927, his eldest son Cory became our host. His own house was nearby but his wife had soon decided that she was too shy to go out, and never appeared at Seend, to Vanessa's envy. Cory himself, though something of a fascist at heart, was kindly and affectionate. He was bullet-headed and bull-necked, but his skin was delicate and transparent, like that of all Bells. His baldness was modified by a fringe of white hair which hung round the back of his head, and his upper lip sprouted a thick toothbrush moustache. In his moss-coloured tweed knickerbockers encircling a slightly protruding stomach he looked every inch a colonel. His small blue eyes almost disappeared when, opening his mouth like a character in a limerick by Edward Lear, he emitted the penetrating sound of Ha, ha, a, a, a, which signalled his presence in any house where he happened to be. To me he was invariably kind and encouraging, and I basked in his presence rather as a sardine flashes in and out of the jaws of a whale.

After dinner, plain but good and nearly always of pheasant, served by the maids in black alpaca with white aprons and caps, we left the gentlemen and retreated to the library. The atmosphere, dominated by Lorna, at once lost any sparkle it may have had: she knew the right thing to say, but said it so that you felt you were eating dust and ashes. I've never known anyone more correct and more abysmally wrong at the same time. When the men rejoined us, filled with ancient port and still puffing their cigars, we were committed by tradition to answering the *Times* quiz, when the superlative memory of the Bells came into its own and they vied with one another in being the first to call out the christian name of Mr Knightley, or the opening phrase of *Sense and Sensibility* – to them Jane Austen was private property.

On Boxing Day the men, with renewed energy, in thick stockings and boots, hung with shoulder bags and guns, tramped off with their dogs to enjoy a day's shooting, thankful that Christmas was over. Occasionally I was allowed to accompany them, and experienced that strange moment of silence in the misty wood, when each man stood in solitude, his gun at the ready, and his spaniel listening intently for the sound of the beater's stick tapping against the trees on the far side. The ground was thick with leaves, and one or two yellow ones still fluttered against the lozenges of blue sky, when suddenly the world exploded, excited dogs yelped, gun after gun went off, and the birds thudded down, their long tails pluming earthward. I earned a few words of praise from Clive for retrieving one of them from under the bushes.

After a picnic of pork pie and lardy cake, we returned to our last evening at Seend. Grandmamma had put on her embroidered chinese shawl, the white fringes of which almost hid her black silk dress. Her hair was piled high in the fashion of the 1890s, stained a faint yellow by the combs that held it in place. On her feet were tiny black leather pumps. Her skin was as soft as down, her lips pleated round the edge as though drawn by a thread. Her pale prominent eyes were very like those of Clive, and her hands so fragile they reminded me of the claws of a marmoset. Communication with her was restricted to scarcely more than 'Good night or Good morning, Grandmamma,' and when she sometimes asked a well-intentioned question, I found it difficult to answer. She survived her husband for many years, living only for her children and grandchildren. She was a perfect example of Victorian repression; if she ever had any egotism it was distilled in selfless dedication to her family. Life had, however, been kind to her, neither giving nor exacting much, and she ended by having faith that she would always be well done by, which in the event was perfectly justified.

One day in London, on my usual afternoon walk with Louie in the Tottenham Court Road, we were both knocked down by a car, whose driver had swerved to avoid something else. I came to to find myself in the arms of a man whose smile I have never forgotten, tenderly handing me into the ambulance. Louie's ankle was broken, but I suffered only from shock, and was liberated from hospital after two or three days, to be greatly petted and spoiled at home. It was for Duncan and Vanessa that the event was traumatic: they had been told by the doctor that I had serious internal injuries, and although this turned out to be untrue, it created a state of anxiety which was often apparent in Vanessa's later attitude towards me. This may have been increased by the fact that soon afterwards, on a visit to Seend which was for once not at Christmas time, I became seriously ill with a throat infection.

These days, such an infection is quickly controlled by drugs, and the normally healthy child hardly experiences illness. At that time, however, the doctor could do little but watch and wait for one's natural vigour to reassert itself. Every illness had its initial moments of malaise together with an inner certainty of imminent collapse and a deep reluctance to admit it. Then there was the relief of going to bed, followed by headaches, pain, nausea and sensations of the strangest kind. On this occasion Vanessa was trapped at Seend while I lay in a state of timeless suspension in the old nursery in the back part of the house. Vague feminine presences hovered round me; Ellen the housemaid and another woman sat murmuring by the fire when they supposed me asleep. Their shadows engulfed the ceiling, while floors and walls no longer seemed solid, but approached and retreated like the waves of the sea. Small objects became large, amongst them my head, stretched to enormous size. Never hungry, I was yet fed from plates with double walls containing hot water to keep the food warm, stoppered with little corks on a chain. So familiar did I become with the garlands decorating their edges that I could easily reproduce their dull green, pink and blue at this moment. The doctor too left an indelible impression: he sprang up by the bed like a jack-in-the-box, jocose in the old-fashioned manner, and yet full of vague menace since he evidently knew too much about me. I didn't like the way he talked to Vanessa, mentioning all sorts of things about my body as though I were not there. Had he been young and smiling I might not have minded, but he was small and stout with a double chin, dressed in black with a stiff wing-collar: he was absurd, but had to be propitiated. One day I made some cotton-wool eggs and, pretending I had laid them myself, I drew them out from under my bottom and offered them to him as the first fruits of my convalescence, though I knew quite well that I should have got better without his help. I remember his astonishment, as though the gesture were improper, and the awkward bonhomie with which he passed it off.

As I slowly recovered, Vanessa came and went. When she was there we shared the morning-room, lighter and more cheerful than any other room in the house. Unable to paint, Vanessa wrote letters or read aloud, or I played solitaire, a game taught me by Grandmamma. It must have been about this time that I saw the huge petals of the magnolia lying on the terrace outside the library; it was cold as I fidgeted there, muffled by my overcoat and talking to Grandmamma inside. Unchaperoned, I would wander off to explore the alleys and paths of the garden, which held a dark charm for me if for no one else. There was even a secret garden enclosed by a wall, with some old apple trees in the centre to which no one ever went, and of which I took possession as though I were queen of an unknown country. Then there was the rock garden, as big as a small mountain with a path running round it just wide enough for me to walk on, putting one foot before the other, and taking care not to tread on its miniature, tufted plants.

Sometimes I was taken to visit the hounds who lived near the stables — a sea of lolling tongues and waving tails, and sometimes to the immense, rose-bricked vegetable garden, its cinder-strewn paths dividing beds of leeks, carrots and cabbages. There were some frames of violets in which I could bury my nose, and the curly chrysanthemums which appeared in the house at Christmas. A whitened glasshouse leant against the wall, containing water pipes which wound their way round like some long-trapped serpent from the age of King Arthur. A fibrous twist of vine knotted itself across the panes of glass, tied with wisps of bast to the wire that was stretched from one end of the house to the other. When it yielded its bunches of grapes, we would no longer be there.

5
Spring in Cassis

In 1927, while in the south of France with his mother and her sister Daisy McNeil, Duncan became ill with an infection diagnosed first as pneumonia, then as typhoid, in those days a much more common and frightening illness than now. Vanessa's anxiety was increased by the fact that she was not on the spot, and had little trust in Mrs Grant's common sense. As soon as she could, she went to Cassis, a small fishing town between Marseilles and Toulon, accompanied by Grace and myself. She rented the Villa Corsica, almost opposite the Villa Mimosa, the much older house where the Grants lived. Just outside the town, the Corsica had recently been built by Agostino, the doctor looking after Duncan, and was barely finished when we arrived. It was a horrible little concrete box erected over a garage, with an outside staircase leading to tiny, hard-edged living rooms with liver-red floors and cream-coloured walls. We were either dazzled by the intensity of the sunlight or, closing the shutters, found ourselves cut off from the rest of the world as though in a snail's shell.

The dining-room of the Corsica was the scene of my first enquiry into sex, which I chose to make during a meal, perhaps an unsuitable moment. Clive, suffering from an unhappy love affair, evidently thought so; his repressive comments provoked my tears and I was led into another dark, womblike room where Vanessa pacified me with a description of the facts of life that, though I hardly remember it, was no doubt accurate. My curiosity had been set alight, but the explanation seemed so abstract that I soon forgot it and felt bewildered at having aroused emotions I could not understand. All I now remember are my fists planted in my eye-sockets and spurting hot, and somehow shameful tears.

At the Villa Mimosa, Duncan's mother and aunt hovered near

him, making access difficult for Vanessa who, never sure to what degree they accepted her relationship with him, felt obliged to exercise all her self-restraint. I was taken to see him, bearded and wrapped in a blanket, staggering rather than walking to meet us. Ethel, his mother, was large and handsome, with a natural warmth and dignity not unlike Duncan's own in later life. In her case it overlay a certain tension, of which one only became aware when one got to know her well. She was somehow out of place among the vine leaves, the hot Dionysian earth, the purple sea and heady scent of pine and mimosa. Her proper environment was an English eighteenth-century house, a pot of tea served in china cups beside a dark, flickering fire, a piece of embroidery in her hands, listening to accounts of her friends and relations. Later, with irritation, Clive called her 'nothing but a memsahib' – but although, naturally enough, she had much of this in her, a certain reserve bore testimony to a greater sensibility than one expects from a woman in such a position. When young she had been a real beauty, with large eyes, an oval face and sleek hair parted in the middle – the prototype of many of Duncan's later paintings. A McNeil by birth, she married Bartle Grant, a grandson of the Laird of Rothiemurchus, whose country seat was The Doune, in the foothills of the Cairngorms. There she met her husband's nieces and nephews, the children of Sir Richard and Lady Strachey, who habitually spent their summer holidays with their grandparents. Ethel, who unlike them had nothing in her of the intellectual or the blue-stocking, impressed them by her serenity and common sense, her ability to calm and render innocuous the rivalries that sprang up within the family.

Though Duncan was born at The Doune, tradition has it that Ethel nearly gave birth to him on the hillside, the idea of which gave him as much pleasure as the truth itself. Soon afterwards Bartle took his family to Burma and subsequently to India, where Ethel was to learn how to become the memsahib that later earned her Clive's unsympathetic comment. She must have acquitted herself well – numerous account books and collections of depressingly orthodox recipes, such as Queen's Pudding and

Chocolate Blanc-mange, testify to an innate sense of duty. Although a timid housekeeper, she was none the less successful in her duties, and an impeccable hostess. More intelligent and sympathetic than most, she and Bartle were both musical, he particularly so; not only did he shine socially, he was a botanist and amateur cook, and reached the rank of major in the army. Ethel was nevertheless conventional, and there were many subjects which one could not mention in her presence. But the fact that she preferred discretion did not mean she was ignorant or condemnatory, simply that she felt that the dangers of exposition might be too much for her. Rumour has it that Bartle was unfaithful to her, and that she fell deeply in love with another major and carried on an affair with him when, re-established in England, they lived near each other in Twickenham. Duncan himself was very discreet on this subject, and it was through Bunny, always incurably romantic about sexual irregularities, that I later came to hear of it.

Aunt Daisy was also, in her own very different style, a remarkable character. Though very like Ethel, Daisy was no beauty. Uninformed by reflection or feeling, her features expressed only energy and a desperate goodwill, as though she wanted to eat you from pure benevolence. She had a beneficent effect on those known as 'the mad', and was often accompanied by someone who was undergoing what might have been called the Aunt Daisy Cure, which it seemed was frequently successful.

It was through her that Vanessa was introduced to Peter Teed, who lived in the Château de Fontcreuse, a miniature château a couple of miles up the valley from Cassis. He owned the ruined shell of La Bergère, a small cottage previously inhabited by farmworkers, to which was attached a story about a miser and a shepherdess, of whom Vanessa painted a picture over the chimney-breast in the dining-room. She paid for the rebuilding of the house, consisting of five or six rooms, and in return was granted possession for ten years, which came to an end at the beginning of the war. The whole family used it, going there at different times of the year. Clive and Quentin enjoyed it in the hot summer months when the town was full of visitors and social life was amusing and, I gather, quite demanding. Vanessa, Duncan and myself went there in the comparative coolness of spring, when our translation from the dark English winter to the crystal clarity of the Mediterranean was a miracle. In spite of the fact that it meant my missing a term at school, we went every year of the first three. I can never forget the atmosphere there, so rich, vivid and varied: the sights, sounds and smells of the South, absorbed when I was still young and impressionable, acquired a power over me that lasts still. I shall always remember being wakened, after an uneasy night on the train, by the intensity of the early morning sun as it shone through my blind, and as I looked out, the sight of the first olive tree, the squiggle of naked vine on the red earth against a clear and glittering sky brought back with a rush the smell of drains in the narrow streets, the powerful voices, the strength and vitality of the people.

No sooner had we arrived than we were assailed by the frantic struggle of the porters who rushed for our bags and suitcases, easels and canvases, unrestrained by Duncan's and Vanessa's remonstrances. Finally, when the taxi had been summoned and we had been packed in with the luggage, the porter had to be tipped, an agony which in those days menaced all foreign trans-actions, and to my acute distress made Vanessa lose her self-possession. Once when we were in Marseilles, seeing something in her face which gave him hope, the porter shouted at her all the way from the train to the waiting taxi, and when in the end she gave him more, she did it with such an abject air that I could not bear it; whether it was worse to see her so weak or so bullied I don't know. I wanted to chase the man away and protect her, but I would rather have seen her stand up for herself. Of this, however, there was no question.

Installed eventually in La Bergère, Vanessa and Duncan were both completely happy, able at last to combine the pleasures of French life with the comfort of being in their own house. Our existence was always quietly domestic, and Vanessa's responsibi-lities scarcely diminished, but the fact that everything was French made it automatically delightful. Vanessa was an ardent Francophile and believed that the French were vastly superior to the English in all departments of practical life: better mechanics, electricians, dressmakers, cooks, better at inventing domestic gadgets, at making easels, stretchers, canvases and paints. So sensible to have paperback books, to dress their children in black pinafores and allow them to stay up late, to have invented the siesta and go to market every day returning with such delicious bread, to have invented champagne, *Petit Larousse* and mayonnaise. She could not say their plumbing was as good as that of the English (those were the days when there was often no more than a hole in the ground and usually a smell of human excrement near one's picnic site), but in every other way they were a more refined race, not least in their sympathy for artists. The fact that the French Impressionists went unrecognised by their compatriots for more than thirty years was forgotten; when she was in France Vanessa felt that she was taken seriously as a painter, not only by fellow artists but by the landlady and the man in the street. It was a sensation she never had in England.

Our cook, Elise Anghilanti, came from the crowded Italian quarter beyond the port; she had a large family, the youngest of whom had been unwanted but was all the more adored. She was brown-skinned and handsome, with the beautiful carriage of those who are used to supporting heavy loads on their heads. She was devoted to Vanessa, who became very fond of her and listened to her stories of woe with more sympathy than she would have given to those of Lottie. It was through Elise that I became aware of the fatalism of southern women who, knowing they are exploited, can only oppose it with the tears and resignation of Catholicism, so different yet no more efficacious than the grim repression of the Protestant. She was an excellent cook, her speciality the traditional *boeuf en daube*. As great a treat was my favourite, *beignets*; she used to dip a gauffering iron first into batter and then into steaming olive oil, then the liberated fritter would slip its moorings and float off to sizzle on its own. At lunchtime, Elise would bring a whole pile of them onto the terrace, where we devoured them as quickly as possible, since they had to be piping hot.

Our landlord, Peter Teed, made wine; from modest beginnings he had become an expert, winning several medals of distinction. A man of warmth and simplicity, he had spent most of his life in India, and as a colonel in the Bengal Lancers had known Aunt Daisy. His eyes were small and dark, rolling in yellowish whites, and his large, bulbous nose pitted, so I believed, with gunpowder; his smile was enchanting, his French accent Churchillian. Completely honest himself, reliable and trustworthy in all matters of business, he deeply relished the subterfuges and sharp practices of his neighbours and rivals, to which he was, rather to their surprise, entirely equal. He lived in the château with Jean Campbell, a New Zealander. They were unmarried – a fact that had to be mentioned to show where one's sympathies lay. As a soldier in a hospital where she was a nurse, Peter had fallen in love with her, and as his first wife wouldn't hear of a divorce they settled in France, where they became highly respected members of society.

Jean, gentle but shrewd, had all the open-handed generosity that one associates with settlers and pioneers. She would have loved children but, for whatever reason, did not have any. Always busy, she was most often to be found in her kitchen, the door of which opened off the terrace, stirring a steaming lake of cherries or quetsches to be made into jam. She also made jars of brandied cherries, offered to her guests after lunch in the cool, dark sitting-room, producing a euphoria only to be cured by a siesta. She was small and slightly lame, and had dark hair which fell in a fringe; from beneath it her calm, friendly eyes looked at me, not without a suspicion of criticism. She allowed me to play round the two formal ponds that lay just below the terrace. Enclosed by slabs of stone, their shallow waters supported innumerable lily leaves on which, with a thud, there occasionally fell a tiny palpitating tree frog, descended from the magnificent row of cypresses which bordered the garden. As I watched, they would change from a dark to a bright green, and with one spring disappear again. In the narrow beds grew multi-coloured tulips, their petals forming fleets of boats which I piloted from one lily-leaf harbour to another.

At lunchtime I would be sent to fetch a jug of water from the Roman spring at the château. Jean once took me into the tunnel hollowed in the cliffside from which the house took its name. The entrance was fringed with ferns, and from the intense heat of the vineyards we entered the cool tunnel, low and dripping with moisture. It pierced the hill for maybe a hundred yards, where it stopped without having found the spring. Instead there was an iron cross, and the water, accumulating, was carried from this symbol of Christianity in a conduit which ended in an unfailing spurt of silver gushing into a stone basin from the gross lips of a pagan god.

Every day Grace would take me and my friend Judith Bagenal to French lessons in the town, about two miles distant. We either walked or were given a lift in the Teeds' old car, or harnessed Coquet the donkey, whose precise but reluctant hooves we goaded in the right direction. After a storm we found on the road quantities of squashed frogs flattened by passing motorists; turned to leather by the sun they were larger than when alive, and we would stand them up against the wall, as Grace said, like preaching clergymen. Once in the town, which smelt strongly of drains and fish, we stopped in a narrow street where, up a flight of stairs, we were welcomed by the intensely respectable Mlle Chevalier, in grey cardigan and laced boots like those worn by the girls of the Folies Bergères. Her mother, white-haired and bunched up in black, was turned out of the room where we had our lesson, and, after our 'Bonjour, Madame,' would disappear into the kitchen.

In the parlour, the table took up most of the room and was covered with a green chenille cloth, which hung in a fringe to the floor, tickling our bare legs. Artificial flowers on the sideboard, florid wallpaper and two thicknesses of curtain made up a claustrophobic atmosphere where, like butterflies, we were pinned down to our lessons. They began with difficult things like verbs and ended with a game of snakes and ladders and a little bribery in the form of sweets. Oppressed by heat, hunger and respectability, we found it more and more difficult to sit still and show the decorum Mademoiselle required. At last, yawning and wilting with excessive concentration, we were liberated and went straight to the pastrycook's where we could choose between *brioches, chaussons aux pommes* and *millefeuilles.* Mme Coulain was dressed like an Arlésienne on a postcard; her sister, with a snowy chignon and transparent white apron over a black dress, had the cheeks of a china rose and pink fingers which curled interrogatively over the buns and cakes. All her life she seemed to have dealt in cream and sugar, and had never married, remaining to help in the shop under the eye of her elder sister. Mme Coulain's son proposed marriage to Grace, and became one of her numerous victims; had she accepted him she would have led a very different life.

One day there was feverish excitement in the town. The air was thick and dark as doomsday. Shop people were rapidly putting up their shutters and others were running for shelter. When we asked what was happening, they pointed to the sea and said, 'Can't you see the waterspout?' I looked and saw three of them, whirling grey columns connecting sea to sky and moving rapidly over the Mediterranean. Boats out to sea were making for the harbour; I was told that if one was hit it would be split in two. As we watched two of the waterspouts smoothly and majestically converging, as though in some ballet of the elements, we were startled by the first fall of rain. Huge drops came down, splashing singly on the pavement, becoming almost at once a deluge. We were hurried into the Coulains' shop and stood looking at the now empty street, which had become a torrent of yellow water carrying with it all the rubbish, sticks and stones from higher up the valley. The violence of the event was exhilarating; Judith and I were delighted when we had to cross from one side of the road to the other on a plank – and at this moment Mr Wyndham Tryon appeared, brandishing a canary-coloured broomstick with purple bristles. He was one of many foreigners who retired to Cassis, where their harmless eccentricities provided the town with plenty of amusement.

Insect life was interesting. The giant moth beating against the window pane, and Nessa in an unusual state of excitement, with her hair streaming down her back, catching it in a jar. There it was for me to see the following morning, its enormous wings closed over its furry body, trying with its velvet feelers to find a way out of its glass prison. Then there were nearly always columns of ants whose activities enthralled us, and once we caught a pair of *scolopendres* or giant centipedes. Julian put these too under an upturned glass and we watched them fight to the death. My attitude was a reflection of my brothers' – a mixture of *soi-disant* scientific detachment and that of the aficionado of the bullring.

If in the Cassis countryside there was no grass and no streams or ponds, there was the pervasive fragrance of woodsmoke, the sudden whiff of rosemary and thyme and the delicious smell of resin. When the wind blew strongly the pines swayed and moaned with self-flagellating pleasure, imitating the sound of the sea, as though they who were rooted to the spot were overcome with longing to see the furthest corners of the world. The little road which ran past the Villa Corsica climbed towards the Couronne de Charlemagne which dominated the town. Beneath it lay the Baie de la Reine, a lonely half-circle bitten out of the pine-waving cliff, carpeted with black straps of seaweed which stuck to one's wet skin and got into the picnic basket. It was like fodder for horses, and we sank up to our ankles in its dry, carbonised straw. Grey boulders clustered at either end of the bay; if one clambered among them one might find shells, dried sea-horses, coloured pebbles or desiccated starfish. Once, to my still-felt shame, I tried to kill an octopus discovered on the beach. Its suckers opened and closed in multiple agony while its arms refused to lie still as, with Julian's help, I piled on stones, trying with youthful inhumanity to shut out its desire to live.

One had to be careful not to tread on the sea-urchins lurking under the blue and purple water. From a boat one could see every wrinkle of sand at the bottom of the sea, tantalisingly visible and yet inaccessible, as though one was staring into a foreign world. Hanging over the side, the temptation to plunge in was strong, and yet stronger still the fear that held one back. Donald Curry, one of the English colony, swam underwater with his eyes open, his white body flashing in the green shadow of the rocks. He seemed more fish than man, whereas we, waiting for our picnic in the sun, were warm-blooded and human, unable to perform such spectacular gyrations.

Back at Charleston my cousin Judith Stephen came to stay. Almost the same age as myself, she was robust, handsome and intelligent; she looked at you frankly and honestly out of blue eyes, one of which was half-brown, reminding me of a collie dog. She was jollier, tougher and more independent than me – hardly a difficult matter since in my case such words were almost meaningless. Nessa said Judith had been neglected, and felt a vague solicitude because she had at least once been locked out of her house and left to roam the streets of London. Either at that time or later she became a pupil of Bertrand Russell, a fact which impressed the grown-ups, though it meant little to me as I had no idea of who he was.

At the time of her visit we were about eleven or twelve, an awkward age. It was summer, sultry and dry. The garden had ceased to be a place of magic, and in any case my pleasures there were private; in the presence of a more adult companion they evaporated. Apart from the temptation to spend money in Lewes, what was there to do? In the presence of Judith, polite and a little shy of her Aunt Nessa, I felt a certain shame at making a nuisance of myself in the studio. Judith had a reputation as a tomboy; at home she spent her time in 'real' occupations, such as sailing the River Blackwater with her father, obeying commands, preoccupied with questions of life and death, whereas I did nothing more vital than dressmaking, or reading one of my Charlotte M. Yonge novels.

I had a sudden inspiration. Surely if Judith could sail boats and command the interest I saw in the eyes of the grown-ups, it was time I grew up! In one of the cupboards there was a hoard of dolls, previously much loved, and it occurred to me that it would be splendid to make a gesture in front of Judith – whether she understood it or not. I brought them out of their oubliette, but a fear of discovery and the resulting questions mushroomed inside me: I decided that the sacrifice must be a secret.

So, on one of those September days when charabancs of holiday-makers forge their way between the dusty hedges to disgorge their passengers at four in the afternoon outside Drusilla's Tearooms, we went to Cuckmere Haven, a gap in the downs where the river emerges from the watermeadows, flowing beside the towpath to the beach. We arrived at about midday, jaded from the heat, our bottoms sore from the scratchy pile of the bus seats, and stood on the road with our two baskets, one full of Lottie's picnic, the other of my dolls.

Watching the bus recede up the hill, I realised I had no idea what to do. The dolls had become a burden, out of place, no longer a symbol of emancipation: impossible to abandon, still more to take home again, pointless to take to the beach. At that moment some gypsy children appeared, materialising like small sharks from the shadows. Embarrassed, though conscious of conferring a benefit, I approached one of the girls and thrust the basket full of rigid limbs and staring eyes into her hands, saying almost inaudibly, 'I thought you might like them.' But the gypsy, probably afraid that she would be accused of theft, refused them and ran off. This was inconceivable, quite outside my capacity for improvisation. Disconcerted, I left the basket on the ground and fled to join Judith, who had remained uninvolved, an onlooker. We trudged off to the beach in a deflated mood, secure, however, in the knowledge that the gypsies were unlikely to follow us.

It was a long day. After a bathe, we spent hours sitting on the large, slippery pebbles, eating Lottie's cake. At last, feeling the cool of the evening on our skins, we set off towards the road, half a mile distant, only to realise that we had lost our money.

Searching for it, we missed the last bus home. For some reason we never thought of telephoning, perhaps because the telephone was still an innovation at Charleston, and in the dark we spent some time finding a taxi. A little light-headed with sea air and fatigue, we rode home in comfort, imagining that the car was emerging from a dark forest stretching behind us to infinity, while on either side the predatory trees were forced to open and let us through.

At last we arrived. Devil-like figures came running out of the house, lit up by our headlights. All at once we understood that we were the objects of anxiety: we were told that Duncan and Vanessa had gone out to look for us, and I knew that Vanessa thought we had been drowned. In the warm and brightly lit dining-room we were given boiled eggs by a concerned and unusually serious Grace. All at once there was the noise of a car, and Duncan was in the room asking for a glass of brandy. He hardly seemed to notice us but hurried out again. My egg became suddenly loathsome and my heart plummeted; I felt exceedingly small.

We were sent to bed without seeing Vanessa, and lay in the studio on our mattresses brought in from the garden because of a threatened change in the weather. Flashes of lightning lit up the square panes of the skylight under which we were lying, and we could see the jagged leaves of the vine. I could see also the tops of the elms where they stood in a row beyond the garden wall. I waited, unable to sleep; after a time Vanessa came in and leant over us, smiling as though she were a goddess from the underworld. I was not expected to apologise, neither did she betray her previous anxiety. Everything was left in suspension. With relief I kissed her, and slept.

6
Langford Grove

Vanessa sent me to boarding school when I was ten – or rather, I went at my own request, after the idea was put into my head by Louie, who wanted to leave us in order to get married.

If I had little notion of what I was letting myself in for, Vanessa, who had never been to school herself, had exaggerated preconceptions, derived more from the novels of Charlotte Brontë than from her own childhood. She instinctively rejected Cheltenham, Neill's School, Bedales or Roedean – each of which, different though they were, had too strong an individuality for Vanessa's liking – and she asked among her friends for a school as little resembling one as possible. She finally chose Langford Grove, near Malden in Essex, which was run by an Irishwoman of character and charm, called Mrs Curtis, or Curty for short.

Vanessa had long ago made up her mind that schools – and education in general – were a waste of time. The best education was assuredly self-acquired, and this was gained after one had left school. I do not know what she expected to occur while one was there, but she set little store by discipline, and hardly more by processes of the intellect. Herself uninterested in knowledge, or in the historical approach to any subject, she could hardly believe that anyone close to her might feel differently. When, as in the case of both Julian and Quentin, it became obvious that they did, she smilingly declined to involve herself, on the grounds of her fundamental incapacity. 'You're so clever, darling, but I'm afraid I can't follow you,' was in effect what she said, and though she never raised a finger to stop anyone doing what they wanted, such an attitude was in itself unhelpful.

She assumed that I would feel the same as she did, and by a gentle persuasion and reluctance to inculcate in me any spirit of objectivity, had made it impossible for me to do otherwise.

Convinced that I was going to be an artist, she decided that I needed no more education than she had had herself. Seeing also that I had showed promise of being good-looking, she thought that I would 'get along all right' without training of the mind: such indeed was her attitude of laissez-faire that one sometimes had the impression that she despised the intellect – or perhaps she only denied my right to develop mine, since she certainly admired the erudition of many of her friends, including her sister. For her own part, she had decided that artists didn't have to think – visual artists, that is, as opposed to other kinds – and it had grown into an ineradicable conviction.

Sending her children to school was therefore more of a practical measure – it would have been very difficult for her, with her professional life to take into account, to do otherwise. The best schools could do was to provide companionship, but she also thought that boys differed from girls: boys needed something tougher and more demanding than she could provide at home. Even so, schools were thought of as a necessary evil, their hardships were to be palliated whenever possible – Quentin, for instance, spent a term of his school life in France. Although I was younger when I started my formal education than either of my brothers, this was simply because I asked for it. I had 'got it into my head' that I wanted to go, and her overriding principle was permissiveness.

Though my desire was only an instinct, it was surely a healthy one. I was aware of the cloying atmosphere that surrounded me, contributing to the disquieting 'difference' I felt between myself and my friends. I did not realise that going to school would not dispel it, given that Vanessa's presence was to pursue me, undermining the whole purpose of the experience. I wanted to find firm ground but couldn't: I was prevented at every turn either by Vanessa or Curty singling me out for special treatment. It was as though some secret agent had hold of me, and, struggle as I might, my feet would never hit the earth. At the same time I was torn between this struggle, which though genuine was uncertain, and the temptation to take advantage of their favouritism. I either

With Vanessa at Charleston, 1928

revelled in privilege or used it to escape situations that demanded some slight objectivity or self-discipline.

The fact that I was pursued by the reputation of my family meant that I became secretly vain, and learnt very little. Thus on the level where I really needed help, school did nothing for me, and one could say that Vanessa's prejudice was justified. But she herself was on the side of the devil, since she persuaded Mrs Curtis to let me drop any subject I found difficult. Latin, arithmetic and allied subjects, games and some other disciplines were successively crossed off my timetable until, in addition to music and the arts, I learnt only history, French and English. True, I would never have shone at any of the discarded subjects, except perhaps for Latin – but it was the demoralisation of not being put to the test like everyone else that was insidious and harmful. I did not realise what it was at the time, but this misplaced permissiveness ate into my morale like a beetle into a honeycomb. If the school had been more intransigent Vanessa would have disliked it – as it was, the school itself aided and abetted her in sabotaging its purpose. She could not believe that I wanted to learn anything – or that, if I did, such a wish was worth supporting. At bottom she felt, consistently enough, that it was all a lot of fuss about nothing.

By the time I had been at Langford for two or three years, Mrs Curtis had fallen in love with Vanessa and Bloomsbury – she was one of the first enthusiasts – and no longer cared whether I was a good pupil or not. I could do no wrong and became the spoiled darling of the school, taking part in nearly all expeditions, concerts, theatricals and so forth at the expense of lessons. Enormously enjoyable, I can't say that it was entirely uninstructive. It was indeed an extraordinary school where one was dragged out of bed late at night to take part in a play by W. B. Yeats; where often, instead of going to church, one was prized out of the brown crocodile of waiting girls to go on a picnic with Curty or to spend the day with her son Dunstan on his yacht. On these occasions we were treated as grown-up only to find ourselves on the following day back in the puerile, competitive atmosphere of a lot of small girls thrown together, out of touch with the outside world. Our venial sins were punished at intervals by Curty who gave us large chunks of 'Lycidas' or a piece of music to learn by heart – and yet we went in fear of her, dreading her corrections, lightly handled though they were. The authority of the other teachers paled beside hers, and though no one ever said they went for nothing, none counted beside Curty. But she, presumably often bored by us, would disappear from view: we never saw her either go or return, but we knew from the general atmosphere that the mainspring of our lives was missing.

Miss Baggs, yellow and scraggy like a Baba Yaga, with greasy hair wound into two plaits on either side of her head, was deputy, and though we supposed she admired Mrs Curtis as much as we did, her ideas of discipline were quite different. She thought that geography and maths, which she taught herself, were important in life, and disapproved strongly when I was permitted to give them up. In class she would look at us coldly from behind steel-rimmed spectacles, 'Get up on your hind legs, children. Who can give me the square root of 21?' We shivered like jelly, but recognised the fact that Miss Baggs cared, and wanted to make us care, about something beyond our laziness and obtuseness, about things beyond ourselves. She fought a lonely battle, however, and her mathematical approach to infinity was no match for Curty's enthusiasm for culture.

Girls whose normal recreations were horses and dogs, point-to-points and cubbing, were discovered to have quite other gifts and were persuaded to take up music, painting and acting. Scientific subjects, never having been taught, were not in question, but excellence at maths or geography now went unnoticed compared with an inclination for drawing or the piano. The walls suddenly blossomed with watercolours by Frances Hodgkin and Miss Fischer Prout, who was occasionally to be seen herself, veiled like a muslim lady, wandering along the garden path or installed at her easel in the evening, her brush dipped in cadmium, painting by electric light, which was her speciality.

Apart from my calf-love for Curty, which dominated the

whole of my time at Langford, I made several friends, none of whom can be said to have lasted into adult life. The most intimate of these was Beetle, who already had a great friend called Cinda. Beetle and Cinda were about a year older than me, and their relationship was that of two Red Indians: they signed their names in blood, kept locks of each other's hair and wore each other's clothes. They talked in a way that excluded everyone else in their vicinity, making it very tempting to insinuate oneself into their society. Beetle was tall, thin, almost gangly, with a dim little face staring from behind a pair of round spectacles. Pale and a little fierce, a flash of wit could suddenly transform her into a grinning imp, and an unsuspected will-power enabled her to exert a capricious authority over others. Cinda was athletic and hand-some – she remains in my mind as a dim but pleasant extrovert. One summer, bathing in the Blackwater, she broke her arm, and was sent home to recover. During this short space of time I became closer to Beetle, and when Cinda returned, a little taller and less tomboyish than before, she accepted me as one of three with perfect equanimity. For myself, I had the pleasure of being a member of an élite, a small group within the larger one where I felt insecure.

We had one glorious week-end when Curty drove us off to Blakeney Point, a bird sanctuary in Norfolk. We stayed the night in a small wooden hut on the dunes, Curty's presence adding to our sense of excitement and privilege. All day we were blown upon by the rough, salty wind; sand was in our hair, our clothes and our food, the noise of the sea in our ears. Birds flew, or rather scudded, rose and dipped from air to water and back again, intent on mating and fishing. They were disturbed by our presence for they had eggs, and screamed incessantly. We learnt to tell terns from black-backed gulls, and these from others; we saw mottled eggs lying untended in little saucers of sand; and for two wonder-ful days we forgot Langford. The world belonged to birds, and we were amazed by their aggressiveness and vitality as they plummeted towards us in protest. Beetle and Cinda reacted with a wild delight that sent them, and myself too, careering down the dunes with our arms spread out, throwing ourselves into the sand only to jump up and rush away screaming with pleasure, until seized with a delicious exhaustion. We felt in perfect sympathy with one another, absorbed by an experience which reduced us to nothing more than grains of sand in the wind. Curty, enjoying it as much as we did, perfectly understood our ecstasy.

Cinda soon left the school, and Beetle became Prima Donna Assoluta. When angry or sad the shadow on her face made my heart sink; her judgments were instant and irrevocable and she carried herself as proudly as a peacock. There was something aristocratic about her which procured her her own way even with the staff, with whom she took the all-or-nothing attitude of the romantic heroine. Wilful and spoiled, she was none the less gifted with an instinctive knowledge of other people's feelings, very far from my own dissociated outlook. It was doubtless this that I found so fascinating and which gave her an advantage over me. Otherwise my only superiority was in being better at music and painting, and I was able to arouse her interest in the latter, so that we were often to be found painting side by side, sometimes on the same picture. She and I were now inseparable, and tried the experiment of asking each other home for the holidays.

She lived with her mother and brother near Edenbridge, in Kent. Her father, a cousin of Mrs Curtis, had been poisoned by eating a crab in the West Indies, which conferred on Beetle the status of an orphan, a condition of which she took full advantage. Mrs Carr was tall, red-faced and kindly, not at all sad in spite of having seen her husband die in front of her eyes. Without much money she did all she could to give her children a good time. Their house, typically Kentish, had tile-hung walls and a gabled roof, set among laurels and privet on the crossroads of the village. In her bedroom Beetle showed me a book by Michael Arlen which was apparently delightfully wicked: in it I read that the heroine daringly touched up her cheeks with lipstick instead of rouge, which made me ponder – what, I wondered, was all the fuss about? For breakfast we had Hovis bread and tea which, different as it was from the thick uneven slices of toast and coffee that we had at home, contributed to my sense of unease in an unfamiliar environment.

Our main amusement was a game of bicycle-polo invented by Beetle and her brother John, played on the crossroads. It was aggressive and skilful, and they were more practised than me, though as my reactions were quick I managed to hold my own in a game that threatened to be one of brother and sister against myself. Mrs Carr presided in the background and provided us with her own kind of entertainment. One afternoon we went to a large and wealthy household, where the young played tennis and the old, whist. As we never played either at home, it seemed to me an extraordinary way of spending a summer afternoon. I was doing my best, however, to hit a ball over the net, when suddenly I felt my stockings slip; making some excuse, I found my way to the lavatory, where I took them off and left them in a corner. When I rejoined the crowd, no one commented on my nudity until on the way home in the bus, Mrs Carr, noticing my long pale legs, started to tease me for being, as she called it, a country bumpkin, making me dimly conscious, almost for the first time, of the exasperation I could cause without meaning to.

At home what did it matter if my legs were bare or my clothes in holes, so long as I was busy and happy? No one ever noticed whether I brushed my hair or cleaned my fingernails – if Mrs Carr had used the word 'slut' she would have been nearer the truth. Vanessa frowned on convention, and we imitated her, mentally elbowing out those who valued cleanliness and tidiness, as though there was no room in the world for both points of view. In our world indeed there hardly was – Mrs Carr would not have survived for five minutes – but no one seemed to think this might be our loss rather than hers. The walls round us were high and the conditions inside the castle odd. Though we were unbrushed, unwashed and ragged, our carpets and curtains faded and our furniture stained and groggy, appearances of a purely aesthetic kind were considered of supreme importance. Hours were spent hanging an old picture in a new place, or in choosing a new colour for the walls. I too would stand in the centre of the studio while a new dress was being dreamed up round me, as though I were a still-life of which the apples and pears were being arranged with careful precision.

To others our narcissism must have been painfully evident, while to ourselves it seemed as though we were exhibiting the purest spirit of objective detachment – in either case it was hardly an atmosphere which welcomed outsiders, and the very fact that we thought of them as such was a betrayal of our attitude. In fact we were almost encouraged to condemn people out of hand as though we had a divine right to judge, and dismiss those who didn't make the grade. We not only got a wicked pleasure from doing it with many of those we called our friends, but also with the dead, artists such as Mendelssohn or the Pre-Raphaelites whom we had decided to despise. I was probably the worst offender, copycatting my elders without their wit, always able to raise a laugh by such means, until one day Bunny, my future husband, said, 'You must stop being so disdainful of those who are unlike yourself.' It was one of those rare occasions when criticism really sinks in, and I *did* stop, as though provided with a pair of brakes.

Vanessa swayed uneasily between the two extremes. It was more from a desire to be friendly and to pass unnoticed, that she did her best, for instance, to dress suitably for Lewes High Street, where she was all but oblivious (or else philosophically resigned) to her lack of success. This hardly mattered, since she was clothed more completely by the formal perfection of her manner than by her moth-eaten coat and felt hat – the combination of the two merely made her more memorable. The regality which so impressed people also kept them at a distance, just as her children's almost flagrant disregard of appearances alienated them. While we thought we were teaching the world a lesson in values, our insensitivity proved something of a barrier even to our friends. Several of mine admitted later that, when visiting Charleston, although welcomed with apparent friendliness, they were conscious of a mass weight of prejudice arrayed against them, which was, had they but known it, not so much embattled aggression as fear of invasion.

My week with Beetle and her family came to an end, and Vanessa drove over to fetch us both back to Charleston. As soon as we found ourselves in the old open car with its splayed bumpers, wobbling like an armadillo across open country, Beetle became morose. She was extremely shy and ill at ease, poor child, even before coming in contact with the family in its entirety, and though Vanessa did her best to be kind she had not the knack of warm simplicity. At all events the visit was a disaster. It rained incessantly, and Beetle, expecting social entertainment of the kind she was used to at home, resisted my efforts to amuse her with painting, sewing or music. In despair I appealed to Vanessa, who sacrificed her time to read aloud Sherlock Holmes, sitting uncomfortably in our bedroom by a smoking wood fire, her voice almost drowned by the noise of the rain on the roof. What a relief when the bell rang for meals and we were able to shed some of our ennui in the dining-room, embarrassingly encouraged by Clive, always hopeful about the 'charms' of the 'young ladies' I brought to the house. Never did Beetle and I visit each other again, though at Langford our friendship remained as close as ever.

Very soon, however, Beetle shot up into maturity; she became pretty, elegant and assured, losing interest in childish things. Curty entrusted her with delicate social missions. It was obvious that life for her consisted of quite other, and so far to me mysterious objectives.

Nevertheless, school was becoming a bore: allowed by Vanessa to evade the exam for which everyone else was working as the crowning effort of their scholastic career, I was simultaneously deprived of this goal and alienated by yet one more difference from my own generation. At the same time I was permitted a certain amount of freedom. I went from Langford to London once a week to join Vanessa and Duncan in the National Gallery on Copying Day, when the public were discouraged from entering by being asked for sixpence. I felt self-conscious standing before Piero's 'Baptism', painstakingly copying the two angels behind the tree. The rare people who did come would sometimes ask me my age – I was fifteen – and one day I found myself pictured in a magazine, looking tall, thin and austere, dressed in clothes more suitable for a woman of thirty, a reflection of Vanessa. (Oddly – or perhaps logically – it was this photograph which, in later days, Bunny kept pinned to the wall of his study.) It was, however, an immense pleasure to be in the cool, calm spaces of the Gallery, surrounded by pictures with which I soon began to be familiar, occasionally strolling round to look at other artists, some of them sitting on high stools, reproducing a famous masterpiece with infinite care.

Back at Langford, both music and the theatre became alluring passions. Louie had been the first to fire my enthusiasm for music, and had taught me the rudiments of the piano. Later I was sent to have lessons with Mrs Smyth, a plump little lady in black satin and a noted teacher of children. I learned to play with fluency, although I never heard a professional soloist until after I went to school. At Charleston all we had was a small selection of records, notably a contralto singing '*Lascia ch'io pianga*', by Handel, and Mozart's Clarinet Quintet, played in the summer evenings while the scent of the tobacco flowers surged in at the open door.

From these meagre beginnings music became of the greatest importance to me. Both Duncan and Vanessa were more musical than they knew. In Vanessa's case it was a gift ruined by bad teaching, whereas Duncan, who had never had a lesson, could play his favourite tunes on the piano, even adding a rudimentary accompaniment. Later, I played duets with his mother Ethel, and had a lively musical relationship with both Oliver and Marjorie Strachey. At school we had what was, for those days, an excellent orchestra, and many week-ends were spent with Curty and her guests singing or playing chamber music. Thanks to her we heard wonderful musicians: the Léner Quartet came to play to us more than once together with Albert Sammons, Emmanuel Feuerbach and a lovely Finnish singer called Lillequist, who looked like a seal in softest black; even, I believe, the Busch Quartet. All came to perform for us at Curty's enterprising invitation. My violin teacher, a German Fräulein and an excellent player, instructed me in the rigidities of an outdated style which did more to prevent than to encourage my efforts, so difficult was it to reconcile making a pleasant noise with what she called a 'good position'. None the less she would sometimes play to us in the evening, filling the hall with sounds of Beethoven, her fingers moving on the fingerboard with the precision of a spider. I would sit rapt, trying to absorb the beautiful movement of the bowing arm, listening to the friction of the bow on the strings. Her skill, so effortless and intimate a part of her – never revealed to me in lessons, where she used to swear at me in German – was something I never tired of, so strange were the vibrations that she introduced me to.

On expeditions to London I was nearly always of the party – indeed on several occasions Curty swept Vanessa into her train and invaded her studio with groups of shy and giggling girls. Always beforehand with the world, Curty took us to see an avant-garde group of actors from abroad. Thus I saw at least three productions of the Compagnie des Quinze, a company organised by Michel Saint-Denis. Michel was a nephew of Jacques Copeau for whom, many years before, Duncan had designed the décor for *Twelfth Night* and *Pelléas et Mélisande*. Of all their plays, I was most impressed by *Noé*, by André Obey, largely because of Noah's double role as a son of God – with whom he talked as though to an intimate, if invisible, friend – and as a father in his own right, to his tribe of a family. I also saw *Lanceurs de Graines*, and *La Loire*, in which the great river was impersonated by an old woman, and foxes and owls conversed together. I identified strongly with Noah, and when we returned to school I took the name part in an improvised production, re-enacting the role with a necessarily fainter flavour of paternal authority but, for myself, great satisfaction. I discovered that I had a stage presence, and enjoyed exploiting it.

It must have been about now that Curty tried to separate Beetle and myself. Our relationship had become suspicious and she did all she could to prize us apart. It was a mistaken insight, as, far from being in love, we were slowly disengaging ourselves from a friendship we recognised as exhausted. All Curty did was to revive a dying flame, and encourage us, from natural perversity, to persist a little longer. Thus, though Beetle was supposed to spend her prep-time in the library where I was not allowed, all I had to do was to invent some excuse for wanting a book, and the sight of me would be enough for her to follow me through another door into the shrubbery, where we would hold long, intimate conversations. It was on one of these occasions that she suggested, on a note of moral superiority, that I was illegitimate, the daughter of Duncan. I was indignant, suspecting from her tone of voice that to be illegitimate meant to be ostracised, but while protesting that I was Clive's daughter, a flash of clairvoyance told me that she was right. There was, however, no more to be said, and I soon forgot about it.

7

At Home in Sussex

Meanwhile life at Charleston continued, bathed it seemed in the glow of a perpetual summer. The household fell into two halves: on the one hand the painters, on the other the writers. If we lived happily together it was largely because, like birds or animals, we each had our own territory, duly respected by the others. Within a domestic framework, rhythmic and reassuring, we all had space and liberty to pursue our own interests, meeting at regular intervals in the dining-room to be sociable and convivial.

Vanessa presided in the dining-room, the magnetic centre of all our thoughts and activities. At breakfast she was always down first, and sat for some time alone, enjoying her solitude. She had dressed and washed quietly, almost secretively, and would be in her habitual place on the far side of the round table, looking with dreamy reflectiveness at the still-life in the centre, or out of the window at the pond and the weather. Her gestures, for the most part slow and even cumbrous, would suddenly reveal her as a girl – virginal and inexperienced. Age showed itself, however, in her furrowed forehead, in the tortoiseshell spectacles balanced on the curve of her nose, and the deep vertical lines between her eyes which recalled that life was uphill, sometimes painful. Nevertheless she was enjoying herself. The luxuries she would have asked for on her desert island would have been a picture by Giotto, and unlimited quantities of black coffee. Now, as she ate a piece of buttered toast with coarse salt and held a steaming cup in long, straight be-ringed fingers, she considered her letters, absorbed the temper of the day, and braced herself to meet its demands.

As always, she was divided: on the one hand she was entranced by what she saw in front of her, on the other worried by her responsibilities. She was faced with half an hour in the kitchen, deciding whether to have spotted dog or treacle tart for lunch,

Clive, Julian, Duncan and Vanessa at tea on the terrace at Charleston, 1932

and listening to Lottie's suggestions, jokes and complaints, which, as she found them irrelevant, she dismissed with a laugh, her hand flying to her head as though she had only just realised the depths to which Lottie could descend. She would have repudiated the idea that, as human beings, the servants were any different from herself, and she did her best to give them as much comfort and liberty as possible, but between them there was a wide gap, seldom crossed, even when she was genuinely fond of them. That she was gentle, patient and self-controlled underlined this distance, as though she were waving from a train to women working in the fields. She did her best, but she could not enter their world, and for them she remained in consequence always a 'lady'.

But a divide of some kind, vague and unadmitted, stood between Vanessa and all of us. In our case it had nothing to do with class, and as she so evidently adored us, nothing to do with love and affection – and yet it had the effect of a seeming lack of sympathy and feeling, a black hole of impalpable depth. She herself was aware of it and would have given anything to cross it, but it affected all of us – those who, like myself, she could not bear to relinquish, and those like Clive, whose hold had slackened in an attempt to remain in touch, for whom she could no longer summon more than a stale affection.

A bad sleeper but of regular, predictable habits, Clive took time, after Grace had brought his jug of hot water and had drawn his curtains, to wash and dress. Unlike Vanessa's, his toilet was a semi-public affair, and he could be heard shuffling on his carpeted floor from bathroom to bedroom – his were the only floors to be completely covered; ours had only rugs, the worm-eaten floorboards showing between – blowing his nose, gargling, brushing his teeth and talking to himself, while a delicate smell of toilet water seeped under the door and one could imagine him stretching out his chin to meet the razor. Finally, pink as a peach, perfumed and manicured but in old darned clothes of once superlative quality, he would enter the room and tap the barometer, the real function of which was to recall his well-ordered Victorian childhood. After greeting Vanessa he would help himself to coffee and settle down with deliberation to eat an orange, dry toast and marmalade.

His eyes, set in shallow sockets under eyebrows that occasionally twitched nervously, were a pale grey, reflecting few of his innermost feelings except his desire to be distracted from the thoughts which had been bothering him during the night. His food eaten, he pushed his plate away and, putting his immaculate fingertips together, made some statement about his plans for the following few days or hours. These concerned friends he had invited for the week-end, the time of tomorrow's train to London, or whether he should pick the apples in the orchard. He was longing for conversation, but failed to interest Vanessa who made it clear that she was bored. Resigned, Clive would at last gather up his letters and disappear into his study, where it was taken for granted he did important work and must not be interrupted.

Duncan sometimes overslept, in which case someone would ask me to play a particularly irritating little *Écossaise* by Beethoven on the piano directly underneath his room. Eventually he would enter the dining-room, growling his dislike of the 'beastly tune', ruffling his hair through his fingers and blowing his nose on a large red bandanna. Insouciant and natural, every day he peeled an orange, ate porridge and drank coffee with fresh appreciation, almost as though he had never done it before, conscious perhaps that each new day was a miracle that might not be repeated. For him, objects seemed alive, never simply things, just as repeated actions never bored him but became a source of reiterated pleasure. After wishing everyone good morning and hitching up his trousers, which were tied round his waist with an old red tie, he would squat to help himself to porridge, kept hot on a low trivet in front of the fire, and tell us about his dreams – often very amusing – or about the book which, tradition has it, he absorbed by putting under his pillow.

On Vanessa's emergence from the kitchen she and Duncan would retire down the long passage to the studio, which was half work-room and half sitting-room, redolent of oil and turpentine. Easels and paintboxes stood about, brushes, sometimes festooned with cobwebs, emerged from jugs or jam jars, palettes and tubes of paint lay on stools or tables, while there was often a bunch of red-hot pokers and dahlias arranged in front of a piece of drapery. The gun-powder-coloured walls were hung with canvases of many shapes and sizes, and some of Duncan's favourite objects, such as a jointed – or rather disjointed – Sicilian wooden horse, a silver table-watch once given by her admirers to Lydia Lopokova, a fan and perhaps a child's drawing, could be seen balanced on the mantelpiece or pinned to a spare piece of wall.

On either side of the large stove were two chairs where they sat, Vanessa smoking the first of her self-imposed allowance of cigarettes, Duncan one of an endless chain always hanging from his lips. Plans for the present and the future were discussed at this time of day, as though life could not be lived until it had been decided exactly how to do it. These included their accounts, left in abeyance perhaps for the last fortnight and now become a mass of small figures jotted down in sketch books and no longer intelligible. When these were sorted out, nearly always to the disadvantage of one or other of them, they turned their attention to higher things: one of them would ask – in a very cool, self-controlled voice – for criticism of a picture in progress. Vanessa would frown and, shading her eyes with one hand while she eliminated a portion of the picture with the other, would try to judge the effect of taking out a line or changing a colour. Criticism never went deeper than this and never touched on psychological issues, but these were the moments when Duncan and Vanessa were closest to each other. Where art was concerned they were united by their differences. Where Vanessa was timid and tentative Duncan would be audacious, and when he was disorientated she would be authoritative. She would straighten out his muddles and laugh at his perplexities, and when, as so often happened, her self-confidence failed her, he would support and reassure her.

When her work was being exhibited, her modesty was genuine and touching. But if anyone criticised Duncan's work she immediately rose up in arms; her fury, her resentment and her desire to protect him knew no bounds. She became formidable, single-minded and ruthless, an upsetting sight to an opponent no matter what his motives may have been. If her sincerity was genuine it was also compulsive, a fact of which she seemed unaware. These were certainly some of the moments in which her feelings got the better of her.

If Duncan was elusive, egotistical and selfish in his love affairs, he submitted to Vanessa in every other area. She accepted this as a mother accepts the faults of a son; her compensations lay partly in the intense pleasure she took in Duncan's personality, partly in the reassurance she got from working with him. It gave her courage to find that her ideas were understood almost before she had made them visible, and that, where painting was concerned, she could often be of help to him. At the beginning, although she found his approach stimulating, she criticised it for being shallow, but later, when she realised how different they were, she often emphasised the gap between them saying, 'I can't do such lovely things as you can,' or, 'Duncan has such extraordinary ideas – things I could never think of.' When it came to her own work, Vanessa deprecated it almost to the point of denying its existence, while Duncan, put on the spot by this tactic, would say it was lovely. Then she would sigh deeply, having hoped for some more profound reaction. The rest of the morning was spent dabbing on the paint, both of them as contented as ducks on a pond.

While painting, Vanessa and Duncan had both developed a technique for carrying on a simultaneous conversation with whoever happened to be there, just enough to assure one of their presence. Much of what was said was almost devoid of thought – a repetition of last week's or last year's conversation, concerned with aesthetic preferences of a simple variety. Duncan, who liked starting hares, might say, 'I've come to the conclusion that Alma-Tadema is a very remarkable painter.'

Vanessa, rising to the bait, would wrinkle her nose and say, 'Duncan, how can you? Of all the vulgar, sugary toads, he's the worst!'

Then I would chip in, asking for a description of Alma-Tadema, and would hear, among other things, how Duncan used to go to tea with his daughters in St John's Wood. Then Vanessa would say, 'It's no good talking about such a degenerate race as the Academicians: what will Angelica say about us when she's forty, I wonder?' Impossible to answer: silence for a minute or two. Then Alvar Liddell's voice over the radio, always on, would announce the Siegfried Idyll. Vanessa would have preferred to turn it off, but Duncan protested, saying he thought there was a great deal in Wagner – finally it was turned down, but becoming inaudible, soon turned up again – the Siegfried Idyll was after all very short and not an opera.

From Vanessa's conversation it soon became apparent that she still believed, as she always had, that subject and even motivation in art had no importance. Crucifixions and entombments, people being impaled or burnt alive, could be looked at for their abstract qualities alone, a blind eye turned to the human content, as well as to the stimulus derived from it that may have affected the artist. Some of this attitude was due no doubt to her dislike of looking at 'horrors', thus perhaps proving the contrary to what she held to be true. It was as though in refusing to see the message she was turning her back on the human element – picking out the currants and rejecting the cake. With Madonnas and children, or Susannah in the bath, she could see them as contemporary nursery or domestic subjects, while happily divesting them of their religion; though she didn't deny that this was at the root of their inspiration, she still didn't believe that it had any 'real' importance. She was unmoved by the fact that a lot of Bach's music is literally figurative – that descending intervals describe the Virgin's tears, or arpeggios the Sea of Galilee. Had one told her, she would have dismissed it as irrelevant. There was a split in her mind as to why things were done, and how; it did not occur to her that the one cannot exist without the other.

Apart from reading books by Virginia and some of her friends, Vanessa read little of what might be called literature – her tastes were almost ludicrously humble. She had read the classics in her youth, but apart from those evenings when she read them aloud to me, never looked into them again. She never read poetry, with the exception of Julian's, and never the avant-garde or the esoteric; what really delighted her were the autobiographies she borrowed from the Lewes Library, written by those whose lives – on the whole unremarkable – disclosed some point of idiosyncratic interest, which amused and sometimes amazed her. She could hardly believe that an elderly lady could spend her life with a primitive tribe in Brazil, or that a married couple, living together, should nevertheless write to each other every day. Vanessa would report on her latest book with a wry humour that betrayed an unexpected interest in other human beings; and though her irony had a tendency to reduce them to little heaps of dust, like snuff, it was not without affection.

Vanessa never went for a walk. If she went out, it was either to shop in Lewes or to find a less familiar landscape for painting. She loved the pearly luminosity of the Sussex light, the pale gold of the stubble fields, the orange-roofed barns which stood in mysterious isolation, and the silver willows whose cool grey smudges relieved the dark, August green of ash or elm. Usually, however, she had no need to go further than the garden to find the perfect motif; she could be seen hovering peaceably in front of her easel, her dress protected by a flimsy French apron, her feet in flat-heeled espadrilles, and on her head a broad-brimmed hat to shade her eyes from the glare. Her presence was betrayed by a smell of oil and turpentine, the colour of her clothes merged into a background of bushes and flowers. Her hesitant, tentative movements recalled those of a sleepwalker or a snail, leaving in its wake a trail of silver.

The studio was the citadel of the house, the sanctuary in which I spent the most treasured hours of my life. It was here, basking in the atmosphere of hard work and concentration, that I felt the most important things would happen; I was a dragonfly that hovers, disappears and returns, a law unto itself. As in a hothouse, I was both protected and stimulated, without a shadow of responsibility. I can imagine nothing better than sitting on the studio floor engrossed in some manual occupation while those patient elders concentrated in their own dreamlike fashion on their art. I absorbed much in that atmosphere that I afterwards valued, aware that it was a privilege to have been there, but it was a little like giving a child strong alcohol – I was drunk with the attention bestowed on me and the expectation so strongly projected that I should behave like a grown-up, while at the same time everyone was ready to give in to my slightest whim. Two dovetailed attitudes were at work, the one born of a tolerance of childish behaviour, the other of a feeling that I should do better not to be a child at all.

At week-ends visitors filled the house: Clive's friends, Lytton Strachey, Francis Birrell and Raymond Mortimer seldom came into the studio, considered by them, one gathered, as a playground where people made horrible messes, and from which

With Clive on the terrace at Charleston, 1925

pictures eventually emerged triumphant. Had it not been for these delectable results the painters would have been regarded as irresponsible, though one might have wondered if that remote though benign trio who spent their time sitting on the terrace in the sun smoking, reading the paper, and gossiping had any right to judge. They were rather like a chorus in an unexciting drama, reflecting on life as it went by, though failing – thankfully perhaps – to interpret its most poignant moments. They exuded a concentrated enjoyment, peculiarly masculine and somehow sacrosanct, as though, before sitting down, they had drawn a circle round themselves in the gravel. Sworn not to disturb them, I would slink past in sandals and sunbonnet to some private lair in the orchard, where their voices and laughter were just audible, a reassuring background to my own preoccupations. Once, when Vanessa was away, I cut myself on a new penknife. Feeling that I was prizing him out of a honeyed retreat, I was obliged to go to Clive for help. He was sufficiently concerned to come with me to wash and bind me up, returning afterwards to his roorkee chair and the meandering, exploratory conversation that constituted his greatest pleasure and was continued from one summer to the next, first at Charleston and then at Lytton's house, Ham Spray.

Of Lytton I remember little – he was for me hardly more than a pair of dark brown eyes magnified by glasses, kindly, but so intensely reflective that communication was almost out of the question. Janie Bussy, his niece, only a year or two older than Julian, was welcomed by all; Clive, the passport to whose favour was good looks, paid her the compliment of calling her a *jolie-laide*, enjoying her wit and malice so much that he forgave her appearance. And indeed she had very beautiful eyes, almond-shaped and almost black, which opened to reveal an intense, secret vitality, as much Bussy as Strachey. Intelligent and tactful, she was nevertheless continuously alert, a merciless observer. Unlike most of our friends, she was elegant, resembling one of those parakeets her father Simon loved to paint, and it was as a painter herself and as a cousin of Duncan's that she was welcomed into the Charleston studio. With Vanessa, who was very fond of her, she showed a tenderer side to her nature, a side that she usually hid under the brilliant badinage which, while it suited Charleston, may have hidden her true personality from other people. Ready to join in any of our activities, she was the perfect *cousine retrouvée*, lost to us for the six months she spent in France every year, returning each spring with the swallows. 'The Bussys are here' meant that not only they but the summer had arrived.

Another visitor was Roger Fry's mistress, Helen Anrep, who after his death continued her intimate friendship with Vanessa. Duncan had first known her in Florence when he was twenty and she was living a gypsy life with her mother, singing to the guitar. Struck by her moon-daisy face and oriental passivity, he said she was his ideal of feminine beauty. Of all our friends she was closest to what in those days was called bohemian, meaning unconventional and penniless. She wore long, flowered dresses pinned at her bosom with a brooch, a shawl dripping from one shoulder, white stockings and little black shoes – rather as though she had stepped out of a picture by Goya or Manet. By nature she belonged to studio life and was no sooner in her chair than the artists once again decided to paint her. She sat contentedly, languidly gossiping in an ironic insinuating manner that I feared and disliked. I did not see the real affection that lay behind it, and it was not until much later when I read some of her letters written to Julian in China that I understood how genuine her sympathy could be. I remember too the impression of real dignity she made on me when, with Duncan, I visited her on her deathbed, no longer laughing at the misfortunes of her friends, simply a frail old woman.

There was however one man about whom I had no reservations, and that was Roger Fry. Equally welcome to both painters and writers, his arrival at Charleston was always an occasion for joy and sometimes amusement, as when, startled by the view of Bunny's aeroplane landing in an adjacent field just as he was driving up the lane, he immediately backed into the gatepost. For the Bloomsbury generation cars were an innovation, and while they welcomed them in theory, they never became accustomed to them in practice, and the machinery appeared to take control of them rather than the other way round. Intent on mastering it, however, Roger treated his car like some continuous scientific experiment, improvising various cures for its unpredictable behaviour with string, elastic bands or anything else that came to hand. Always uncaring of the impression he made, he was a myth and a source of myths, leaving behind him a trail of disbelief and amusement which his friends would magnify into a shape larger than life. If at times his demands were exorbitant, he replenished our spirits with some mysterious elixir and stirred our summer boredom to a new interest.

To me he was a grandfather with paternal and avuncular overtones, whom I had no qualms in asking to perform miracles. Thus he would teach me to tie knots designed never to come undone, make for me paper birds that flew, stick things together for me without the faintest sign of impatience, his deep voice purring gently, a forgotten smile hovering over his features. His attitude to making things was very different from that of Vanessa and Duncan. Duncan was like a child: his nails and glue were made of faith, and if this failed he simply laughed. Vanessa was more practical – indeed the curtain rods she hung from twisted nails and bits of string are still in place at Charleston – but Roger had theories and had to prove them, so that everything he made for me had the double fascination of being a game for me and an experiment intended for his own satisfaction.

In a suit of pepper-and-salt tweed, slightly bent at the knees, Roger was always in an attitude of absorbed curiosity, his rather large features almost unstrung from eager participation in whatever was going on. His fine white hair, parted in the middle, gave him a feminine appearance; his nose, larger than life, his teeth strong, the cleft in his chin deep – he recalled the wolf in *Little Red Riding-Hood*. His eyebrows were tufted, while beneath them his eyes lived in vital intensity behind gold-rimmed spectacles. His voice trembled, like a double bass, with a thousand shades of feeling and intelligence, together with the pleasure of

Roger and I, 1928

being alive. Aware as he was of all the complexities and subtleties of art, he himself appeared to have no hidden corners, no reservations, and this, while it made him both vulnerable and attractive also, on occasion, made him difficult.

I did not know then that Roger and Vanessa had been lovers, although I could not be unaware of the special consideration with which he treated her, the intimacy mixed with deference, and his way of listening to what she said, almost as though he still hoped for a message that had gone astray. Although she basked in the glow of his extraordinary vitality, she was frequently exhausted by it, uninterested in his latest enthusiasm, on which she was liable to pour cold water. And when it came to criticism of her and Duncan's painting, always one of the necessary ordeals of Roger's visits, she was silent with inexpressible reservations. Her habit of keeping her most intimate feelings to herself meant that they took on an unavowable importance, and it was only after the much-loved but unsuspecting Roger had gone that Vanessa felt free to laugh with Duncan over all he had said. They resisted Roger's influence – but it was very hard to deny its existence.

It was to Roger that I owe my first taste of asparagus; he brought bundles of it down to Charleston, having obtained it cheaply from some unusual source. I had made up my mind to dislike it simply because everybody was so concerned I should do otherwise, but when it appeared on the table, limp rods of jade and ivory, I allowed him to persuade me to try it – and then, naturally, could not have enough. He nearly always brought something with him – on one occasion a paper kite in the shape of an eagle, on another a matchbox decorated by himself with a small piece of jewellery inside. I remember his sensuous feeling for objects, and the passionate quality of his interest in the subject of the moment, blind to all else.

When I was very small, I was invited to tea by Roger at Dalmeny Avenue, in London. Several other little girls were there as well as his bearded, deep-voiced sister, Margery, who kept house for him. Expecting the spread of jellies, cakes and biscuits that were usually put before children, we each sat down to a plate bare of all but a baked potato. Discovering that these were made of cardboard, everyone but myself burst into tears. Somehow aware that this was what the grown-ups called a joke, I opened mine and found it filled with hundreds and thousands, multi-coloured sweets the size of a pin's head, impossible to eat without scattering them all over the floor – indeed impossible to eat at all. Dismayed that their attempt to amuse us had fallen so flat, poor Margery bustled away to get the real tea, hidden behind a curtain, and the rest of the evening, no doubt spent more normally, was forgotten by me.

It was on a summer's afternoon in 1934 that Clive, coming out to find me on the gravel in front of the house, told me that Roger had died. He told me no details, only hugged me so tight that I could scarcely breathe and certainly could not ask questions: my one desire was to get away from his suffocating grip, which seemed actually responsible for this dreadful news, and held no comfort. It was the first death I had experienced, and the unreality of it left me disorientated. The last time I had seen Roger he was alive and perfectly well – now he had disappeared; I was told that he had died, and I should never see him again. I knew that absences were painful, but it was impossible to believe in one that would last for ever . . .

Vanessa was at Monk's House, with Leonard and Virginia, and when the news came she fainted. I don't remember her return to Charleston, but the following day, on going near her bedroom, I heard her howling in anguish. The door was closed, and it was beyond me to open it – indeed I dared not, almost fearing that the creature who made those noises could not be my mother. I fled from the house, and walked far over the fields before I could persuade myself to return.

One day, while looking for a pen or pencil on Vanessa's desk, I came across a letter from Helen, describing how Roger had slipped on the polished floor, to lie there for a long time until he was found, and how in hospital he had died of pneumonia, unconscious of what was happening – and I felt the healing comfort of reality, the certainty that no one was trying to shield me from the truth – I was free to make of it what I could. Helen had written part of her letter upside down, which somehow symbolised her state of mind as nothing else could have done. Trained not to read other people's correspondence, however, I felt a certain shame at mentioning my discovery, and a possible source of understanding between myself and Vanessa sank without trace.

8

The Woolves

Our intimacy with the Woolves, as we called them, was close in spite of the fact that the atmosphere we breathed was very different. We were a family, whereas they were a couple, ranging through life with single-minded commitment. To them we, the younger generation, must have seemed disorganised and undisciplined, even egotistical, battening on to Vanessa and stretching her to the utmost. At the same time Virginia loved finding herself back in a family environment, and, feeling that an afternoon at Charleston was a holiday, her main purpose was to twang the strings and make them buzz with teasing and laughter. To her this was the breath of life, and she thoroughly enjoyed it. For us it was as though a stopper had been taken out of a bottle – criticisms, questions, and jokes poured out of her: we were exposed not only to her realms of imagination but to a mind as tough and sharp as obsidian.

Neither Virginia nor Leonard pretended to be other than they were; there was no facile morality or talking down to children – on the contrary Virginia was less remote than Vanessa and insisted on a reciprocity that filled the air with tension, which if sometimes alarming, was also stimulating. She was convinced that I inhabited a world of fantasy special to myself, and she longed to enter it. In this world she was Witcherina and I, Pixerina; we flew over the elms and over the downs, our main object, as far as I remember, being to bring back fictitious information about other members of the family. As may be imagined, this suited Virginia to perfection, for she loved inventing improbable situations in which Julian, Quentin or Vanessa might find themselves, whereas I, dazzled by her virtuosity, remained wingless, fixed to the ground.

It was at teatime that I remember Virginia's arrival at Charleston, pacing through the house, followed by Leonard and Pinka, the spaniel, whose feathered pads would slap on the bare boards beside her master's more measured footfall. Virginia, seeing myself and Vanessa sitting by the fire or under the apple tree in the garden, would crouch beside us, somehow finding a small chair or low stool to sit on. Then she would demand her rights, a kiss in the nape of the neck or on the eyelid, or a whole flutter of kisses from the inner wrist to the elbow, christened the Ladies' Mile after the stretch of sand in Rotten Row, Hyde Park, where Vanessa in the past had ridden on a horse given her by George Duckworth.

Virginia's manner was ingratiating, even abject, like some small animal trying to take what it knows is forbidden. My objection to being kissed was that it tickled, but I was only there to be played off against Vanessa's mute, almost embarrassed dislike of the whole demonstration. After a long hesitation, during which she wished that some miracle would cause Virginia to desist, she gave her one kiss solely in order to buy her off. Although she felt victimised and outwitted by her sister, she won the day by her power of resistance, and an utter inability to satisfy Virginia's desires, which completely disregarded Vanessa's feelings. She suffered mainly because, much as she loved Virginia and deep though her emotions were, she became almost unbearably self-conscious when called upon to show them. Of her love for Virginia there was no question: she simply wished that it could have been taken for granted. They were both affectionate, but Virginia had the advantage of articulateness, which Vanessa may have distrusted, having suffered from it in the past: Virginia's flashes of insight into other people's motivations could be disturbing. In one word she could say too much, whereas Vanessa, priding herself on her honesty, was inclined to say too little. Neither could Vanessa compete with Virginia's brilliance and facility; made to feel emotionally inadequate, she also imagined herself lacking in intelligence. She distrusted Virginia's flattery, in which she detected an element of hypocrisy, setting her on a pedestal for false reasons, but she did not see how to retaliate without brutality, of which she was incapable. She became more and more truculent, her exasperation masked by an ironic smile with which she tried to discourage Virginia's efforts to extract a sign of love.

When the ceremony of rights was over, conversation resumed on a gossipy, joking level, flavoured by Virginia's wit and Vanessa's logic. Once Virginia had been liberated by receiving her allowance of kisses, she became detached, quizzical, gay and intimate. Vanessa, let off the hook, relaxed the knot into which she had tied herself, and although she continued to feel waves of frustration and reserve, the hedge in which she sat, and which Virginia had been trying to break down, grew less thick and impenetrable.

Leonard, like a vigilant and observant mastiff, remained unmoved by this behaviour. He was made of different material from the rest of us, something which, unlike obsidian, couldn't splinter, and inevitably suggested the rock of ages. I know from later conversations with him that he strongly disapproved of the way in which I had been brought up, and although, had I been his own daughter, he would not have used the rod, neither would he have spoiled the child. I remember two incidents which, trivial in themselves, gave me a taste of his authority – a taste which suggested a different set of values. Once, not realising the nature of my crime, I spilled some type that he had just spent hours in sorting, and I said nothing about it. A week later I was reprimanded with a controlled annoyance which seemed to imply a standard of behaviour I was seldom expected to live up to. On another occasion, having asked for a copy of *Flush* to give a friend, I was unprepared to pay for it, but Leonard made me go home and get the money. These contacts with a sterner reality impressed me – he seemed to be the father figure who was missing in my life. And yet, had Leonard been my father I would have resembled one of his dogs, never beaten but always intimidated by the force of his personality.

For my birthday one year he gave me a splendid Victorian copy of *Pilgrim's Progress*, filled with pictures of Christian marching onwards in stiffly engraved wooden drapery. For some reason this book meant a great deal to me, and my eyes met those of Leonard across the festive tea-table in a moment of intense understanding I seldom experienced. For once I felt limpid and transparent, purged by emotion of all the dross of puerile secrecy and prevarication that usually submerged me. I had unwittingly come into contact with the passion in Leonard's character, which was both convinced and inflexible, contrasting with Vanessa's tendency to compound and procrastinate in favour of those she loved, and Duncan's ability to laugh away and ignore things he didn't like. They were conscious of a moral force in Leonard which they repudiated as narrow, philistine and puritanical. Both he and Vanessa were natural judges and both were full of prejudice, but whereas she avoided morality, Leonard clung to it, always remaining something of the administrator of the Hambantota District in Ceylon. In Bloomsbury, vowed to amorality, this may have seemed a little heavy-handed and irritating, but with it went a refreshing purity which in later years I fully appreciated.

Once every fortnight in summer we would bundle into the car and, in the chalky stillness of a Sussex afternoon, drive over to Rodmell, crossing the Ouse at Southease level-crossing. Monk's House, in the heart of the village, was, very largely for this reason, as different from Charleston as possible. The house was long and narrow: the rooms opened out of each other in succession, the whole house lower than the garden outside, so that one stepped into it rather as one steps into a boat. Plants and creepers knocked at the small-paned windows as though longing to come in, invited perhaps by the green walls. Cool and peaceful, on a hot summer's day the house seemed to bubble gently, like a sun-warmed stone that has been dropped into a pool. As a little girl I had sometimes stayed at Monk's House as a guest, and once my cousin Judith and I had discovered the amusement of rolling down the steep lawn opposite the front door, only to be scolded by our nurses because we were bright green all over. Green is the colour that comes to mind when I think of the house and garden, with its curling fig trees and level expanse of lawn overlooking the water-meadows. Green was Virginia's colour; a green crystal pear stood always on the table in the sitting-room, symbol of her personality.

For tea we sat at the long table in the dining-room, the only big room there was. Virginia, sitting at one end, poured out tea, not as Vanessa did, with a careful, steady hand, but waving the teapot to and fro as she talked, to emphasise her meaning. Our cups and saucers were of delicate china, our food less solid than at Charleston — there were biscuits instead of cake, farmhouse butter procured by Virginia herself, and penny buns. Virginia ate little, popping small pieces of food into her mouth like a greyhound. Before tea was over she would light a cigarette in a long holder, and as her conversation took fire, she herself grew hazier behind the mounting puffs of smoke. She would describe a visit from Hugh Walpole or Ethel Smyth, or some local scandal, and, encouraged by our comments and laughter, rise to heights of fantasy unencumbered by realism. From Julian and Quentin in particular the laughter became ecstatic, their chairs tipped dangerously backward, hands raised in mock dismay at Virginia's audacity or slapping their thighs in capitulation. Her brilliance was not without malice, and her eyes shone with delight at her success. While her mind seized on the unconscious, weaker and more vulnerable aspects of people, noticing details of behaviour with a brilliant haphazard appropriateness that skirted the edge of the possible, Leonard would wait, and then describe the same incident in terms that were factual, forthright and objective. Not that Virginia was not capable of objectivity, but she arrived at it by a different road, and on these occasions flung it over the windmill, intent only on enjoying herself.

When the meal was over we all trooped into the garden, invited by Leonard to play the ritual game of bowls. If the first half of the entertainment had been Virginia's, the second was his. He took charge of the game, pressing everyone to play, even the least experienced, who were given handicaps and praised if they did better than expected. Leonard paced the doubtful distances with large, thick-soled feet placed carefully one before the other, sometimes attended by Pinka, who adoringly sniffed each mark on the grass, only to be gruffly told to go and lie down. Leonard's word was law, his judgment final, and we would continue with the gentle, decorous game while he carried on a discussion with Julian or Quentin about the habits of animals or local politics.

Meanwhile Virginia sat in a deckchair under the elm tree, smoking, talking to Vanessa about cousins seen again after many years, and laughing about them in their own quiet, throwaway fashion, like two birds on a perch. Alternatively, Virginia, unable to tolerate boredom, did her best to inspire rivalry between Charleston and Rodmell, preferring to squabble about houses rather than remain silent. Vanessa hated the thought of life in a village, and, albeit reluctantly, defended the liberty and privacy of Charleston, where we were a law unto ourselves, where no Mrs Ebbs looked over the garden wall or called out to one on one's way up the village street, and where there were no church bells to intrude on one's Sunday afternoon. But when I went to sit beside them Virginia would insist on trying to make me say that Rodmell was the superior of the two. In the end I would become impatient and she would say, 'Oh! Pixerina, what a devil you are! But you do love me, don't you?'

'Of course I do, Witcherina, but I can't lie to you.'

As I grew older and she grew richer, Virginia made herself responsible for my dress allowance, which was £15 a quarter, quite enough for clothes and minor pleasures. Although the money was hers, Virginia had often forgotten to bring it with her and had to ask Leonard to pay me by cheque. It was a little like extracting water from a stone. Although Leonard did not protest, he went through a process of finding and putting on his spectacles, which made him look like a hanging judge, plunging his hand into some inner pocket to draw out his cheque book, then his pen, from which he unscrewed the cap with some difficulty, and finally writing out and signing the cheque with a trembling

With Virginia at Rodmell, 1932

hand in complete silence – all of which seemed a test of my endurance. In the end he handed it over with a half-smile, like the flash of a needle under water.

Leonard and Virginia's relationship was above all comradely: deeply affectionate and indivisibly united, they depended on each other. They knew each other's minds and therefore took each other for granted – they accepted each other's peculiarities and shortcomings and pretended no more than they could help. They were bound together by honesty. There was little, if any, conjugal bickering. Leonard never failed in vigilance and never fussed; neither did he hide his brief anxiety that Virginia might drink a glass too much wine or commit some other mild excess; he would say quite simply, 'Virginia, that's enough,' and that was the end of it. Or, when he noticed by the hands of his enormous watch that it was 11.00 in the evening, no matter how much she was enjoying herself, he would say, 'Virginia, we must go home,' and after a few extra minutes stolen from beneath his nose, she would rise and, as though leaving a part of herself behind, follow him and Pinka to the door.

Once I remember walking behind Virginia up the garden steps, when it suddenly occurred to me to wonder whether she had ever made love with Leonard. I assumed she had, and yet it seemed impossible – I could imagine her in bed with no one, in spite of her obvious femininity – but no doubt the absence of sexual feelings was an important factor in the success of their relationship. Virginia remained a virginal, bony creature, stalking her way through life, like a giraffe. And yet, though her head was often above the clouds, her feet were firmly enough planted on the earth. Shabby, untidy, wispy, her fingers stained with nicotine, she cared not a straw for her appearance, but by some curious fluke remained both distinguished and elegant.

On one occasion I went to tea at Monk's House when Virginia was alone. Before the evening was over she complained of a headache and I helped her to bed, finally leaving her alone to await Leonard's arrival from London. It was the only time I ever saw her near a breakdown. I had been shielded from knowledge of these, partly because Virginia had needed protection when she was suffering from them. But there was also a common family habit of referring to Virginia's 'madness', which made it seem quite unreal – and, as though that were her intention, it became something one could not contemplate. Seeing her suddenly threatened left me with the impression of a stoic vanquished only for the moment, as brief a moment as she could make it. In spite of her fragility Virginia had enormous resilience: she could never resist the call of life itself, no matter what shape it took. She never cut herself off from people, as we did at Charleston; even if it threatened to destroy her, human contact was indispensable. She searched continually for satisfying relationships, finding for the most part only volatile if stimulating contacts in a sea that threatened to submerge her, and which, had it not been for Leonard, would have done so.

With hindsight I can see, though she never said so, that Virginia was disappointed in me: she wished I was more intelligent, more disciplined, and probably agreed with Leonard about my education. She would have liked me to have had more enterprise and independence, to have been less predictable. Longing none the less to seduce me, she succumbed to the more conventional ploy of trying to improve my appearance, doing things which did not come naturally to her such as taking me to my first hairdresser, giving me jewels and feminine knick-knacks. But she also gave me her copy of Mme du Deffand's letters, presented to her many years before by Lytton, and encouraged me to talk to the Rodmell Women's Institute on the theatre, helping me with my script. She tried to probe and loosen my ideas, and, when she forgot to be brilliant and amusing, showed a capacity for intimacy which I found illuminating. At such moments her critical faculties and insight were used intuitively, and never made one feel inferior. I felt too that there was in her a toughness and courage to which she clung through thick and thin, of which one was aware under all the jokes and laughter.

9
Looking up to Julian

Anxious to go to Italy before the heat became too severe, Vanessa took me away from Langford after Christmas 1935, without entering me for the school certificate; I was barely sixteen. We travelled to Rome in the unaccustomed grandeur of Vita Nicolson's chauffeur-driven car, accompanied by Quentin. After a few days at the Hassler Hotel, just off the Piazza di Spagna, we found a studio in the Via Margutta, traditionally the artists' quarter. Our landlord was a Fascist and a bully; we had some trouble with him, the cause of which I forget, but which left Vanessa both crushed and indignant. We were conscious of our official unpopularity owing to the sanctions imposed by the British Government, and occasionally Mussolini made a speech, while once or twice we saw Blackshirts stepping down the Corso. This was the extent of our contact with the Fascists: those we saw most of, the shopkeepers, peasants and the odd painter, showed no political feeling. It was more disturbing when our washerwoman burst into tears; she had heard nothing from her son in Abyssinia for six months. This was one of the occasions when Vanessa's shyness prevented her from showing sympathy. I remember standing there, longing for her to embrace the woman, to show some human warmth, but she held back, troubled and awkward; in spite of our enthusiasm for the southern temperament, we could not free ourselves from our inhibitions.

When Clive arrived for his usual continental holiday, he took me with some friends to picnic on the shore of Lake Nemi, and from there to visit the Princess Bassano in her country house. The young Prince showed me the stream that ran under it, swift, deep and cold, brimming with weeds of an intense and brilliant green. Preoccupied but full of dignity, the Prince was preparing to join his regiment in Ethiopia. Under the sophisticated façade of our fellow guests was a barely perceptible malaise which, had I been better informed and more politically sensitive, would have held a greater significance.

On the whole, however, we escaped confrontation with the régime, and continued unalarmed in a hermetic but enjoyable existence. Vanessa and Quentin painted every day in the Forum or in the Medici Gardens under the ilex trees, while I wandered in the sun or sat on a tomb learning the part of Juliet, for it had now been decided that I should go on the stage, and I immersed myself not only in Shakespeare but in Bram Stoker's life of Henry Irving and any other books I could find in the English Library. Every morning, evading with some difficulty the lecherous old men on the bus, I went to have lessons in Italian with Signorina Boschetti, who seemed to have had as a student every English girl who had ever been to Rome. There I pored over Italian verbs and the most famous of Dante's sonnets, unable to concentrate, my thoughts drawn inexorably to their own secret but well-worn paths. The mornings, however, were taken care of; it was the afternoons that were dangerous. After the siesta there were dozens of youn men hanging about in voluptuous attitudes, waiting for the innocent and untried female. One afternoon, as I stood on the Pincio, I was invited by a handsome stranger to ride in his carriage drawn by six white horses: my imagination, nourished on *Romeo and Juliet*, plus a command of Italian hardly strengthened by the boredom occasioned by Dante, probably jumped to unwarranted conclusions – this charming young man was very likely referring to the horse-power of his car. Vanessa, when I told her, seemed quite unmoved, though to tell the truth, walking alone round Rome at the age of sixteen was not without peril.

At a loss to find a music teacher, Vanessa was pleased to meet her old friend George Booth, whose daughter Polly was studying the 'cello; she recommended a violin teacher, to whom I took my Handel sonata. No sooner had I played a few bars than he whisked away the music and substituted a page of formidable arpeggios. They seemed entirely without attraction and continued, like the Ganges, for ever. Every mistake, whether of bowing, notes or fingering, was drily, mercilessly corrected, and by the time I was half way through I was exhausted. It appeared I was wasting my time playing at all. The stuffy atmosphere of the maestro's apartment was oppressive, and, as I travelled home with Vanessa inside the bus, tears coursed silently down my cheeks. Aghast, she suggested that I have no more lessons; the old pattern was repeated, my pride and self-confidence eroded. She wrote to the violinist saying that we were unexpectedly leaving Rome. Ten days later we met him in an antique shop in the Via del Babuino: awkwardly, we retreated behind a statue until we could unobtrusively leave the shop. No doubt we laughed about it afterwards, but I was secretly mortified by my failure.

Duncan arrived at last, and took another studio in our building, from the roof of which we could see far out over Rome. He continued to work on his decorations for the liner, the *Queen Mary*, for which he used me as a model, while in the evenings we sat in the marble interior of the café Greco drinking grappa, teasing him about various relationships with virginal spinsters supposed to be in love with him, while half-hypnotised by our reflections in the sombre perspective of the café's mirrors. Afterwards we strolled home in the warm evening air past the theatrical decor of façade and fountain.

Finally we decided to hire a car and tour south to Naples, Pompeii and Paestum. We included the cascades of the Villa d'Este as well as those of Caserta, and stopped at every village market in the hope, often realised, of buying pottery or seductive if tattered pieces of silk and brocade. The weather became oppressively hot, and every evening, after a day spent in the back of a closed car, I suffered from an excruciating headache. Fearing Vanessa's solicitude, I tried to hide my pain, and by the time we had seen the sights and eaten the inevitable stodgy spaghetti, my one desire was to collapse on my bed. We seldom if ever stayed in a good hotel, indeed probably there were none. Our lavatory was usually a stinking hole in the ground, and hot water was difficult to procure. One night I woke to see Vanessa in the bed beside me, searching for bugs by the light of the candle. Their squashed bodies decorated the walls, but I was fortunate in providing no temptation either to bed-bugs or fleas. I fell asleep again with a vision of Vanessa looking surprisingly young, her nightdress slipping off her shoulders, and a twist of silver hair falling down her back.

On our return to Rome Vanessa found a letter from Julian waiting for her; he had accepted a teaching job at the University of Wuhan, near Hankow, and was leaving for China in a month. Though not completely unexpected, this news was a shock to Vanessa who had probably not dreamt that China – four to five weeks away by boat, to her a country unknown and almost unreal – would be Julian's objective. She at once packed our things and set off for England, amazed and perhaps disappointed to find that I was in a state of excitement, not at the thought of saying goodye to Julian, but at going down to Langford for the last two days of term. The temptation of flaunting my newly found independence was too great to be resisted.

In London I found Julian in a state of euphoria, shopping for topees and tropical suits, deciding on which gun and which books to take, as though he were going to be away for a lifetime. There were also friends and girlfriends to be bade farewell, whose claims he balanced one against another, like a juggler. He filled London, which in those days seemed far smaller than now, with his high spirits, responding with enthusiasm to the idea of going to the most foreign of all foreign places, hoping that the change would grant him a new lease of life. His greatest regret was at leaving Vanessa, whose fears and apprehensions he well understood, while she on her side tried to sympathise with his feeling that it would do him good to get away; the immense distance he was to travel symbolised the importance he attached to breaking away from so much that he loved and valued. It seemed as though the liberty which Vanessa had always appeared to offer was allowed only on the understanding that he would never take advantage of it, feeling that if he did she could not bear it. And yet, though this was in part the impression she gave, she also encouraged him to go; the intellectual part of her personality was in favour of individual liberty, while the emotional clutched desperately at her favourite son.

For Julian it was a supreme effort to gain his freedom, without if possible hurting his mother. He could not doubt, however, that he did cause her pain, but although this gave him a certain anguish, it could not quench his curiosity and enthusiasm. His love for Vanessa remained paramount: no other woman would come near her. She and he were more like lovers than mother and son: one had only to see him leaning over the back of her chair, and the quality of the smile on her face, to be aware of this. From China he wrote her a series of descriptive, informative and intimate letters, and she always looked forward to their arrival with longing. In one of these he says: 'I'm far more devoted to you than I've ever been to a mistress, and indeed so much so that I should find it very difficult to marry because none of my friends and mistresses can begin to compare with you.' Vanessa would read them aloud to us with a pleasure that betrayed her hunger: she missed a companionship that had steadily been growing closer. She viewed his departure rather in the light of a personal tragedy, which left her, if only temporarily, bereft and desolate.

Of all our personalities Julian's was the warmest, the least reticent and the most courageous. Generous in spirit, he made friends easily in spite of a certain shyness; he could often be socially clumsy, but his contemporaries were attracted by his physical vitality and irresistible sincerity. Young for his years, his mind was filled with an amalgam of ideals and prejudices which lay down unhappily together, and he longed for greater experience to stabilise and orientate him. His adoration of Vanessa, which may have given him a greater understanding of women, did not make life easier for him, because the freedom he constantly struggled for was always in jeopardy. Imbued with the ideas and attitudes of his parents, for many of which he felt a deep sympathy, he was reluctant to relinquish a way of life that in many ways suited him, but he felt compelled to test it against his

Julian, aged 22

own discoveries. He thrashed about, like a fish too big for its pond, trying to find deeper water.

For me his departure to China was rather like desertion at a moment when I particularly needed his understanding. It was in him alone that I found the imagination without which at that age one languishes; although he was still young, I trusted him, and I believed in him. He understood more than anyone else the effect of Vanessa's dominance on the one hand, and of Duncan's passivity on the other. He was indeed more aware of my predicament than I imagined, and wrote from China to tackle Vanessa about her possessiveness, thinking that she stood in the way of my sexual maturity. It was a considerable effort of courage and imagination; the effect it had on my life was negligible.

From Vanessa's reply, ten pages long, it is evident that the arrow hit its mark. Discursive and subtle, much of what she says is plain common sense and some of it, quoted by Frances Spalding in her biography of Vanessa, is moving; but she reiterates her denial of possessiveness with a desperate desire to impose her rationality, like someone continuing to talk in an effort to drown the voice of doubt inside them. As I read it again, I feel the almost unbearable weight of her personality and the extraordinary sense of suffocation that resulted from so much fuss, when all one wanted was to be left alone.

It is true, however, that before he went abroad Julian's own attitude to my sexual education was curiously confused. He veered from warmth and intimacy to behaviour that was painfully dismissive, as when he sent me from the room in order to discuss sexual subjects with a contemporary of mine whom he judged more sophisticated, or when he said – perhaps teasing me – ' "Be good, sweet maid, and let who will be clever." ' Although this roused me to fury, it didn't prevent me from responding to him when we walked round the lawn by moonlight, talking about my vague and amorphous aspirations. It was his capacity for focussing his attention that was so extraordinary; no one else listened with such fullness of concentration, thus showing his own delicacy of perception and convincing me for a moment of my own validity. His occasional lack of sensibility was merely due to clumsiness; I learnt much from the warmth of his embraces, which resembled those of a lover and were exactly what I needed. I had seen little if any physical contact between my parents, no sharing of a bed or kisses snatched at odd moments, and I was deprived of sensuality; as a consequence I was, in spite of a hidden preoccupation with sex, deeply repressed. Both Duncan and Vanessa and Leonard and Virginia were, as couples, asexual if not virginal, and unable to initiate me, and there was something about Clive's well-meant overtures that repelled me. Julian's tenderness was therefore all the more important and all the harder to lose, especially at a time when I was on the threshold of my own sexual adventures.

I was lively, flirtatious and I think affectionate, with, like Virginia and Vanessa, an intense longing to be loved. I was not entirely stupid, but I was uninquisitive, timid and blinded by the egotism which, I think I may truthfully say, I had always been encouraged to manifest: I was insensitive to the needs and feelings of other people. My unbalanced flights towards independence were mere emotional flashes in the pan, unsupported by thought or reflection. Some strength of purpose I must have had, but even now I am unable to say what it was. I was very conformist, I might even say imitative, an attitude at first unconsciously encouraged by Louie, and then, finding myself unavoidably dominated by my mother, I was by the same token unable to imagine anything more original than actually becoming a second Vanessa. It is indeed only fairly recently that I have been ready to admit or recognise the profound differences between us, and how in reality I am more Grant, and perhaps McNeil, than Stephen.

However that may be, I was in those days moody, easily deflected, easily provoked either to tears or to laughter, without even a skeleton sense of values. Or rather, perhaps I should say that I never succeeded in sticking to my values except by default, or a refusal to engage myself more positively: my ideals were too youthfully intransigent to be adaptable to real life. None the less my instincts leant towards honesty and truthfulness, making me realise dazedly that my first obligation in these matters was towards myself. But emotionally, though sensitive, I was undeveloped. Weighed against those of other people, my feelings, even to myself, seemed to count for nothing. I had to nurse them in private to convince myself of their validity, and was unaware that this was the worst mistake I could have made. I lacked the ability to remain true to myself through thick and thin, in spite of the fact that I often appeared to other people as obstinate and intolerant – but this was a mere smokescreen, like the ink of the cuttle-fish. I was in reality a ready victim, and once I had been knocked down was unable to regain my balance. I was easily demoralised, and my need for affection led me to practise self-deception and subterfuge in order to get it. Any strength and resilience that might have accrued from a warmer relation to Duncan was simply not there, and as a result my sexuality, nourished on romanticism, was of an unbelievable fragility, hardly calculated to attract young men of my own age – though I did have some admirers. It was more that I was only partially attracted to them: unfortunately I never fell in love with one of them.

Though I was indifferent to such things, I could not remain unaware of Julian's political activities; neither was I completely insensitive to the menace of the international situation. I said nothing, but was frightened, and hardly reassured by the noisy and animated discussions which took place between Julian and his friends on the lawn at Charleston. I was not expected to join in, and had I done so it would, I felt, have been rather like jumping into an electric mixer. Ten years older than myself, brimming with ideas, articulate and well informed, Julian's friends terrified me partly by their intellectual brilliance, which seemed to leave no room for gentler feelings, and partly by their view of the world at large, which appeared to dismiss the human element as of no account. I did not realise that this was prompted by the condition of the world itself, and that they were sincerely concerned about the future: I simply failed to recognise it through the glitter of words and phrases.

I was horrified by the glimpses I got of a world where individuals counted for nothing and were simply the pawns of powers who themselves were struggling to supersede each other. Incapable of objective questioning or assessment, stricken because I instinctively realised that listening to these young men involved saying goodbye to childhood, I retreated from the scene they conjured up. In the light of their conversation, even those things which appeared most solid and unshakeable were threatened. In the growing sense of anguish even the sound of an aeroplane was ominous. Never again would we know those calm country silences, when all noises were either animal or human, when the sound of a tree falling two miles away defined the distance between it and ourselves, or the twittering of a lark in the sky measured the spaces of blue air above; even the mechanical hum of the threshing machine called forth a sympathetic echo from the empty, sunbaked fields. Now these sounds were rapidly becoming drowned by the noise of car, lorry and aeroplane, never, in the foreseeable future, to be silenced. Lying in the grass listening to phrases about bayonets and fifth columnists, Hitler and Fascists, I froze, like a mouse, in my place, hoping that these terrifying images would pass me by.

The next year was in many ways an exciting one. For the first time in my life I found myself living away from home, in a foreign and highly sympathetic environment. Julian gone, I went to Paris to live with some friends of the Bussys with whom, as one is apt to do in those years of one's life, I fell deeply in love – a love affair of friendship that has lasted to this day.

François Walter, handsome and bearded, was a civil servant and at the same time a left-wing agitator for peace, editing a paper called *Vigilance*. At the threat of a *coup d'état* by the *Action Française*, François learnt to shoot with a pistol, lending our lives a quality which in England would have been termed overdramatic but in France seemed merely realistic. Zoum, his wife, came from a family of Belgian artists, and she herself looked like a figure from a picture by Georges de La Tour, dignified, ample and superb. She too was a painter; her easels and canvases were to me a familiar adjunct of life, although her paintings were quite unlike any I had seen before. Deeply in love, she would become desperately anxious if François were late for supper, and hang out of the window on the sixth floor, hoping to hear the sound of his taxi. When he eventually returned, he was bitterly reproached and then passionately embraced before being given a delicious meal. Immediately afterwards François would plunge into editing his paper, pacing up and down the apartment until far into the night, sustained on minute cups of black coffee.

To me such scenes were a revelation of the possibilities in human relationships hitherto suspected only through literature. Zoum's mother Jeanne, there on a long visit, attracted me less in spite of her motherliness, as, imbued with the spirit of gallic common sense, she tried to brush away the cobwebs of my nordic shyness. Shocked at my ignorance of the mechanics of sex, which she discovered one morning after a thorough questioning in the kitchen, she did her best to enlighten me; but I closed my ears to the information she offered. Neither did she improve our relations by sitting on the other side of the double doors when I was practising my violin, shouting at intervals, '*Angelica, c'est faux!*' These trying shrieks affected me like a violation: I felt that my faults should be left to me and my violin mistress.

It was Zoum who was my second mother; her robustness, kindness and sense of humour never failed me, even in years to come. I was amazed by her combination of masculine intellect, emotional warmth and sensuality, which I had never met before. She too was a dominating personality and I fell completely under her spell. Her husband, François, was on the contrary all nervous intellect, refined, objective, trained to dismiss all save the one fact that mattered. Deeply attracted, I was at the same time nervous of drawing his attention to myself, happier when he paid me none, and yet thrilled if he ever did so. Certainly these four months in Paris were a time of being fully alive, and of learning much that was new; a time of intensified interest that has remained a yardstick ever since.

On my return to London in the spring of 1936 I went almost immediately to the London Theatre Studio as a pupil of Michel Saint-Denis, whom I had last seen as Noé in the Compagnie des Quinze. I eventually got to know him well, as our friendship continued both during the war and after, when my children, then small, caught his delighted attention. As a student I was lost in love and admiration for him, seeing in him a Zeus-like father figure for whose good opinion I craved. As far as age went he was barely old enough for such a role, but in knowledge of human nature he was singularly cut out for it.

At first his appearance was unimpressive; without being fat he was short and fairly solid, almost stocky, usually dressed in unremarkable grey tweed. It was when he was seated that one became aware of the nobility of his forehead, completed by the curve of his aquiline nose, on either side of which was a pair of shrewd, hawklike eyes. His mouth, from which usually hung a curved pipe, was full and sensual; he spoke with a strong gallic accent, and a cogency that carried complete conviction.

With us, his students, his relationship was largely avuncular, although it could on occasion betray a sadistic element. In spite of his difficulty with the language, he had all the articulateness of an actor, having at his command every means both of persuasion and compulsion. We were as wax in his hands. He could on occasion be chillingly and even cruelly ironic, a mood against which we had little protection especially if, like myself, we were willing victims. Nevertheless, he was a remarkable teacher, and, as I now think, a great man, deeply cultivated and with interests outside the theatre which enriched his productions within it. Since his death he has been either ignored or condemned as a crank, but his was a rich personality, impregnated with emotion and sensibility in addition to a powerful intelligence; and to him the theatre in England as well as France owes a debt of gratitude.

As at Langford, my progress at the school was qualified by Michel's respect for Bloomsbury. My career there began well: I was a tree in a mime-play about Orpheus; but it continued on a downward path, although not without moments of success.

When, for example, I played the part of one of the heroines in a comedy by Dryden, Michel told me that for five minutes I had succeeded in acting – 'You *can* act!' This was a red-letter day, its greatest merit being that, not having put it to the test, I can still dream that it might have been true. Michel was always particularly kind and charming to me, but his treatment of me as someone 'special' added to my sense of unreality: I felt like a paper doll trying to enter an alien world. When he finally rejected my interpretation of Irina in *The Three Sisters*, I was both hurt and confused. For reasons of his own he had given me very little help during rehearsals (on which, unusually, he had chosen to bestow his personal direction), and I now felt as though, without explanation, he were reversing his previous attitude towards me. I hid my feelings behind a show of indifference, which even he was powerless to penetrate.

In spite, or perhaps because of, the growing threat of war – as though the light while it narrowed also grew brighter – life in London was very pleasant. Vanessa, Duncan and I lived at No. 8 Fitzroy Street, now destroyed but then one of those mid-nineteenth-century houses with large rooms and heavy cornices, whose lower floors were occupied by Drown's, the picture restorers, while the upper regions were allocated to various tenants. I had a room at the top which, though it looked on to the street, was reasonably quiet. In it I did everything except eat and have my bath; these functions were carried out in Vanessa's studio, which was built out at the back, and reached by a long narrow passage bridging the gap between it and the rest of the house. Roofed with corrugated iron, it trembled and shook underfoot, heralding the approach of our visitors with a rumble as of stage thunder.

Vanessa and Duncan's studios stood back to back, the mirror image of each other. From the little window in Vanessa's kitchen one could see the legs and feet of Duncan's guests tramping in single file along the last length of passage, at the end of which stood an empty, hooded porter's chair, made of straw. A small door then led into the vast studio, whose magical, dusty space was lined with matchboarding, and called to mind the rehearsal rooms of Degas' ballet dancers. First occupied by Whistler, then by Sickert, the place was a refuge from the progress of time and from the encroachments of modern life; it was made for the dreams and visions of the artist, floating, it seemed, in the London fog caught and held there since the nineteenth century. What wonderful, lofty and mysterious places they were, full of the paraphernalia of the artist, in each case so characteristic. Among the easels and models' thrones, encrusted palettes and jars full of brushes, rotting still-lifes and the smell of turpentine, stacks of dusty canvases and saucers of drawing-pins and pieces of char-coal stuck together with varnish, Duncan had reserved a small island by the fire where there was a square piano on which his friend Mrs Hammersley or Harriet Cohen would play. A couple of guitars hung on the wall, faded but sumptuous textiles were flung over the bed where numerous cushions suggested the harem, lit by a lamp made from a piece of African sculpture. What could be more delightful for his friends than to sit there smoking, drinking and talking, conscious of a quality in the air they could find nowhere else?

Vanessa's studio was divided in two by some long, embroidered curtains seldom drawn but delimiting one half as the working space while the other was our dining-room. There we ate on a heavy octagonal table whose surface was sheeted with aluminium; it never lay quite flat, and our knives and forks slid from hump to hollow as though on a metallic sea. Behind the studio a small room functioned as both kitchen and bathroom, dominated for a few hours each day by the gaunt and noble figure of Flossie, who did both the cooking and the shopping.

It was at this time that my adoration of Duncan was at its peak, If, at the age of six or seven, I had chosen him as my 'husband' in preference to Clive, it was probably because I felt instinctively that he was my father; but it was also because he was younger, more approachable and more gentle. He was never didactic, he never bullied, and seldom offered advice unless it was asked.

Many people, afraid of seeming insensitive, exaggerate their emotional reactions. Duncan never did so; neither did he appear to repress his feelings, but remained intimately in touch with his instincts. Considerate and good-mannered, there was a sense of proportion in all he did. So long as he was able to paint, he seemed to have no egotistical impulses, and yet one always felt that he did exactly what he wanted. At the same time he was always ready to experience anything new, and had an elasticity of spirit that to me was like champagne, delicious and invigorating. Vanessa distrusted this quality, assuming that if he gave way to every temptation he would never do any work; but not only did he work as hard as anyone I knew, he lived for his painting as though it were a lover.

Duncan acted as a buffer between myself and Vanessa. I do not really know when my feeling of malaise with her started. I am tempted to say it had always been there – and indeed that is not impossible. Children are naturally guileless, and, although they cannot speak of it, immediately detect hypocrisy in others. I am certain that Vanessa felt guilty with regard to me, and, whether she would have admitted it or not, betrayed it by small, almost imperceptible signs. In addition, unreasonable though it may seem, I resented her age – less for the years it represented than for her lack of elasticity, both physical and moral. I needed a punch-ball to try my strength on, but if I hit out my fist encountered nothing but cotton wool – and I immediately felt ashamed of my violence. Such experiences are disorientating because it is natural for the young to want to be strong, but I could never even get into training. Much of my later weakness was due, I think, to learning not how to control myself, but how to repress my feelings. It was this attitude too which glued me to Vanessa's side when I should have been out exploring on my own. But in Duncan's presence her power to depress and make me feel inadequate evaporated. With her, I was like a boat stranded; when Duncan appeared, I floated free. When he was out in the evening, Vanessa and I would sit in the studio waiting for his return, each of us longing to hear his key in the door. He would arrive ruffling his hair and smiling, to recount his evening's experiences – and for both of us it was a release.

Sometimes Duncan and I would go to a party together, leaving Vanessa by the fire. These occasions were a delight, if a trifle unnatural, since I should surely have been accompanied by some young beau. They nearly always ended with Duncan as the last guest, reluctant to go home because he was so much enjoying himself. Sometimes, however, it was they who left me behind, and I remember one such occasion when, after dinner at the aluminium table, Vanessa sat in the studio, reluctantly but patiently allowing herself to turn blue under the practised fingers of the actress Valerie Taylor, who was covering her face with grease-paint. A fancy-dress party must have been the reason for this metamorphosis; Vanessa ended by resembling a leaden Venus about to mount her plinth of stone.

Our weekly family meetings continued to take place in Clive's flat in Gordon Square. Duncan, Vanessa and I strolled round there from Fitzroy Street, familiar with every brick and every paving-stone on the way. Traffic was negligible; it was more like a walk in a country town than the sky-scrapery, rock-hard metropolis of today. Bloomsbury seemed to have changed little since the days of Thackeray and Dickens, with street after street of Victorian houses, shabby, down at heel and hardly comfortable since they were too tall and narrow, but still full of domestic life and interspersed with shops that catered for the needs of the inhabitants. Vanessa would dress in something long and flowing with shawl and earrings, and, emerging from her strange, barnlike studio, would walk slowly along the pavement leaning slightly forward, more from apprehension than eagerness. Duncan, a cigarette hanging from his lips would tell me stories of how in Gordon Square he was once struck on the tongue by lightning, or of how, when Maynard was away, he helped himself to two entire crates of Moët et Chandon.

Lottie, as thin as a string bean, her lips a raspberry red, provided us with a meal worthy of a *cordon bleu*, and after dinner we sat in Clive's bachelor apartment, his sitting-room filled with books, comfortable chairs and a sofa, and shaded lights glimmering in the smoke of cigars. Here we listened to Virginia's excited and unbridled accounts of her long flirtation with Sibyl Colefax, or her more recent one with the Comtesse de Polignac. The pleasure of each occasion, for herself and the others, lay not only in itself but in a recreation of the past, a homage to friendship and affection. Like magnets, they still attracted each other, eclipsing all other friends in each other's company. The past was so inextricably mixed with the present and so full of incident and emotion, and their minds and thoughts so well known to each other that every allusion, however slight, was caught and understood, every joke appreciated: communication was a luxury to which no effort attached.

It was here that Vanessa read aloud Julian's letters from China, describing a world which, however vivid it was for her, for the rest of us remained hard to imagine, although each member of the family, including Quentin, who was occupied at this time with political projects, wrote to him keeping him informed of events in England.

Eventually, after about a year and a half, Julian came home, resigning from his post at Wuhan University partly as the result of an amorous indiscretion, partly because he could no longer ignore the Civil War in Spain. He had grown thinner and was changed, and so was I. We were at first strangers to one another, attempting clumsily to rediscover our earlier intimacy. But there was not much time; all too soon he succeeded in persuading Vanessa and his friends that he must fight, although out of consideration for her he consented to go as a Red Cross ambulance driver rather than to the trenches. Once more there was a period of preparation, coloured by Vanessa's unspoken anguish together with the usual anxieties of getting the necessary permits and equipment, enjoyable perhaps for Julian but for no one else. Vanessa accompanied him to Newhaven, and after what seemed an incredibly short space of time, he was gone – London was emptier.

Appropriately enough, I was dancing at the London Theatre Studio in a dramatic ballet on the theme of Goya's '*Desastros della Guerra*'. It was my most successful part and one I very much enjoyed. In June that year we gave a fortnight's showing to friends and public. One evening after the performance had started Duncan suddenly appeared in the narrow alleyway outside the theatre: Julian had been killed, would I come home immediately? Trembling, I climbed the ladder leading to the lighting platform from where Michel watched all our shows. Seeing something serious was wrong, he immediately came down with me and, hearing what had happened, put his arm round me. Of course, if someone else could take my part, I could go home.

I found Vanessa in bed, white and swollen with tears, almost unable to speak. I said I had known all the time that it would happen, and so did she, but apart from that first embrace we became no nearer to each other. Everyone's effort was strained towards her, longing but unable to comfort her. Only Virginia and Duncan were of some use to her. Although not a mother herself, Virginia was imaginative enough to understand the kind of agony Vanessa was going through and was unafraid to talk of the past. Duncan, as usual, preserved his extraordinary serenity. Clive, however, pretended to a distressing detachment at a moment when detachment was impossible.

Before long we were at Charleston again, and Vanessa lay on a daybed in the studio looking down the empty garden path, occasionally weeping, more often exhausted. It was decided to publish a book made up of Julian's letters from China and other writings with contributions from such friends as Maynard and Bunny. Vanessa slowly turned her attention to reading, writing and choosing, which, melancholy though it was, was better than the inactivity that had so far incapacitated her. In spite of Julian's recommendation, in a letter she was to receive after his death, that she should work, it was some time before she stood at her easel again. Slowly, however, she reoccupied her place in the household, fulfilling her previous duties in an effort to restore a normality to which we had all grown so accustomed that we could hardly recognise life without it. The effort she made must have helped her, but nothing could restore her previous confidence in life which had been born of a feeling that, doing no harm, we should not suffer much. Although to a large extent she shared Julian's beliefs, she was in no way consoled thereby for his death; her best resource, apart from work, was to focus her attention on her remaining children.

10

Child of Two Fathers

I remember that summer as endless, hot and tiring. One day when Vanessa was better she took me into the drawing-room at Charleston and told me that Duncan, not Clive, was my real father. She hugged me close and spoke about love: underneath her sweetness of manner lay an embarrassment and lack of ease of which I was acutely aware, and which washed over my head like the waves of the sea. It is hard to say what prompted her to tell me just at that moment – how much was due to a plan conceived long ago, and how much because of her actual state of emotion. It is very likely that she felt, however obscurely, that she owed this gesture to Julian's memory. Not only would the knowledge she was about to impart help me to mature, but he would approve of the honesty of her gesture. At the same time she must have felt an immense need to unburden herself of the lie we had all been living under for the last seventeen years. Anxious about how I was going to take it, she said it need change nothing, since it was the intimacy of the present, not the facts of the past, that was important: my love for Quentin, for example, need not be affected by the fact that I now knew he was my half-brother. I remember the curious little shock this assertion gave me and I recognised the fact that I did indeed love him, though never before had I thought of saying so, which may indicate what an undemonstrative family we were. Although Julian had written to her that I was even more emotional than he was himself, I was not an outgoing child. If Vanessa expected me to show surprise at her information, she must have been disappointed: I hardly batted an eyelid, though when she left me to myself I was filled with euphoria. It was a fact which I had obscurely known for a long while. Whatever explosion there may have been occurred far below the surface: at the time I simply felt that a missing piece had been slotted into place.

Still, I did not talk to Duncan: perhaps I was afraid he would deflate my exultation. I preferred to gloat alone, unable to overcome my feeling that, with such a father, I had been marked for a special destiny. I was the little girl, red rose in hand, who falls in love with the prince, the hideous and charming beast. It never occurred to me that I was fantasising a Duncan that could never be. Nor did I realise, in my desperate need of a father figure, the true nature of my sacrifice. I should have spoken to Duncan. As it was, Vanessa said no more, he said nothing, and I remained closeted in dreams.

My relation to Duncan never got beyond this: I adored him, but the will to be his daughter was all on my side, and was received with no more than a bland serenity. It was an asexual barrier of simplicity and kindness which baffled me. I could not see round it, but – I cannot now help wondering – was there anything further to see? Assuredly there was, but it was too nebulous, private and self-centred to respond to the demands of a daughter. As a result our relationship, though in many ways delightful, was a mere simulacrum. We were not like father and daughter. There were no fights or struggles, no displays of authority and no moments of increased love and affection. All was gentle, equable, and superficial – it was indeed his ability to remain uninvolved that made him such a delicious companion. My dream of the perfect father – unrealised – possessed me, and has done so for the rest of my life. My marriage was but a continuation of it, and almost engulfed me.

So absolute was my confidence in their wisdom that I never thought of blaming either Duncan or Vanessa for their silence. Even later, when my resentment fell upon Vanessa, I never could bring myself to blame Duncan. This was years afterwards, when I had begun to realise what I had missed, and how deeply the ambiguity of the situation had sunk into me.

Although Vanessa comforted herself with the pretence that I had two fathers, in reality – emotional reality, that is – I had none. It was impossible to associate Duncan with any idea of paternity – and he never tried to assume such a role. Clive acted better, but carried no conviction, for he knew the truth. How different it would have been if we had all acknowledged it. Among other things, Duncan might have been able to show what affection he had. Vanessa never reflected that perhaps he too was inhibited by her prevarication, just as she never realised that, by denying me my real father, she was treating me even before my birth as an object, and not as a human being. No wonder she always felt guilt and I resentment, even though I did not understand the true reason for it; no wonder too that she tried to make it up to me by spoiling me, and in doing so only inhibited me.

As a result I was emotionally incapacitated – though it would be a great mistake to think that, had she told me before that my father was Duncan, my life would have been easier. My difficulties might indeed have been much the same, since his character would have remained constant. It was knowing the truth, instead of being deceived by those who had not fully considered the consequences of their lie, that would have changed everything.

But curiously enough, when the moment came, being told the truth made the world seem less and not more real. No one seemed capable of talking openly and naturally on the subject: Vanessa was in a state of apprehension and exaltation, and Duncan made no effort to introduce a more frank relationship. They gave the impression of children who, having done something irresponsible, hope to escape censure by becoming invisible.

Even Clive did not profit from my recently acquired knowledge; I was told by Vanessa that he preferred to look on me as his real daughter, and that therefore I had better say nothing to him. This was a great pity since Clive's affection was based on something better than pretence, and his relief at seeing all the cards on the table would have led to an easier relationship between us. He would have understood, if he wanted to, that there was nothing to prevent him from thinking of me as a daughter, while on my side the very real affection I had for him might have been released.

Whether Clive was aware of it or not, my attitude to him was deeply affected by the ambiguity of the situation, and because I could see Vanessa's feelings for him. I did not examine these at the time but I now understand that, while outwardly composed of trust and respect for his knowledge of the world, and an affection from which all effervescence had departed, she had, in expecting him to maintain a pretence, ridden roughshod over his finer susceptibilities. Did she never consider what was to happen at the moment when I appealed to him *as* my father, when I expected from him a moral support that he knew himself to be in no position to provide? Had anyone pointed this out, I think Vanessa would have said that, since Clive himself knew the truth, he had only to show his affection for me – without admitting that a permanent state of prevarication exacts its own dues. She might also have said that, had I been more precocious and more sensitive, she would have told me of it earlier, thus reducing the risks of an appeal to Clive. But she appeared to ignore the fact that, apart from and beyond affection, his answer would have been deprived of authority, and that it was this that I longed for, if only in the end to reject it.

Vanessa imagined that she herself could shoulder the entire situation, but although this was meant well, it was a gesture compounded of arrogance as well as generosity, and showed blindness, if not indifference, to reality. It would be easy to say she failed to recognise the importance of the relationship between father and daughter, but I do not think this was so – she evidently hoped that the one between myself and Clive would be fruitful – but she may not have understood that a daughter longs to be possessed by her father, and this Clive was in no position to do.

He did, however, show a greater sense of responsibility towards me than Duncan – although my general insecurity prevented me responding to it wholeheartedly. I suffered from reservations which I attributed to his inherent coldness, or to certain innuendoes and implications to sexual subjects, which I found embarrassing. Within certain limits, however, we got on very well, although as I look back on our relationship I regret that, at the time, I did not do his intentions justice.

Clive had welcomed my arrival in the world with generosity, and had continued to show a warm interest in my existence, even on rare occasions taking Vanessa's place when she wanted to go away – something Duncan never did. Of course, Nellie or Louie was always there, but as a point of reference, Clive was reliable, calm and good-humoured. When, as a very small child with mumps, appositely and without tears, I said, 'Oh dear, I've fallen out of bed,' he was delighted at my natural philosophy, and repeated the story at intervals for the next twenty years – a reiteration which irritated and blinded me to the affection that lay behind it. I remember too an occasion when I was rude to him. I was still small, but old enough to know what not to say, yet my tongue, like a lizard's, seemed to act on its own, and I came out with something now lost in the limbo of the unconscious – some remark met on his side with a blank surprise, a disbelief which showed that he was wounded, although I never heard any more about it.

On another occasion, having reached the age when Seend no longer seemed the magical place it once had been, I asked Vanessa whether I need go there for Christmas. She referred me to Clive, and with some trepidation I went to see him in his study at No. 50 Gordon Square, where he sat in his cane-backed chair puffing his pipe. Although innocent of all desire to cause pain, I have little doubt that my manner was tactless: young as I was, I did not realise that he was and always would be fond of a place and people that I, with youthful inconsistency, had just rejected. Clive looked at me over his spectacles in silence, and I knew that his feelings were hurt. Diplomatically, however, he promised that, if I went to Seend this year I need not go the next. For me it was a milestone because, even if he did not realise it, it was the first time I had talked to him as an adult, capable of doing something from choice rather than because I was told to.

If Clive had ever suffered embarrassment from our fictitious relationship, he seemed determined to disregard it now that I was growing up. For him, well-off, living half his life *en garçon* in London, it was a delight to give me my first oyster or plover's egg, and introduce me to his cosmopolitan and society friends, with whom we would lunch at the oval mahogany table, sitting long into the afternoon under the influence of still champagne, the remains of purple passion fruit crushed on our plates, our words left floating in the air. Clive enjoyed showing me off. He was also, however, sensitive to my predicament, and knowing that Duncan was incapable of showing an interest in my sexual education, gave me *Daphnis and Chloe* to read – pastoral and poetic and perfectly adapted to my stage of development. As my French improved he gave me *Manon Lescaut*, followed by the rather curious choice of *Les Liaisons Dangereuses*, which, as I might have known, was a Bloomsbury favourite. It was thanks to Clive that I became an enthusiastic admirer of Mérimée, enjoying *Carmen*, *Colomba*, *La Vénus d'Ille*, and some of the *Lettres à une Inconnue*.

It was only much later that I realised Clive was an unhappy, even a pessimistic man whose gifts had never been fully realised. One has the impression that with his friends – whose standards, though high, were also limited – he had never quite passed the acid test of being 'first-rate'. Whether this was because his literary achievements were lacking in distinction or his attitude to his love affairs hysterical is hard to say, but as time went on their criticism had its effect, and with some bitterness he recognised its justice. Together with a quick intelligence, his undoubted talents were for the observation of humanity – to which he brought the gift of common sense as well as a certain cynicism – and for the armchair variety of enjoyment, to which the more chairs that could be added, the better. Although Bunny has pointed out that his generosity was founded on selfishness, yet he was a man who preferred to enjoy himself in company, who always welcomed the unexpected guest, and who gave without stint. He loved his friends to exhibit themselves, to be what he expected them to be, and although no doubt this put a burden on them, and tended to limit their intercourse, it was a disarming form of affection: in his presence they could not help responding to his benevolence.

More than any other member of Bloomsbury, Clive was socially experienced, suave and competent, partly as a result of having money, but also because of his longing to associate with those whose style of life needed money. Unlike Vanessa or Virginia, he was unafraid of the refinement and delicacy of manners natural to the rich, although he did require a certain degree of culture and beauty to go with them. Characteristic of him though this was, however, one sometimes got the impression that his own delicacy was lacking; he so longed to impress by means of elaborate witticisms, flattery and *double entendres* that he was embarrassing, and in the end his friends were charmed more by his transparent goodwill than by his eighteenth-century manners.

There were in Clive two men, and both were at least a century out of date: one was the man about town, the dilettante, and the writer; the other, the squire, the countryman, and the sportsman. In the latter role he was, I think, more genuinely at ease, since his knowledge, skill and love of country life dated from childhood. In neither character did he quite fit into the world as it was, and one of the things that one loved him for was his refusal to recognise this, his ability to transform his surroundings either into the haunt of a sybarite or into the property of a landed gentleman.

At Charleston, where he had no property, he walked about the country as though he owned it, and the shepherd, the game-keeper, the gardener and their wives were devoted to him. If this assumption irritated Vanessa, she got her own back not only by a certain coolness but also by her ability to suggest that she might, at any time, act in such a way as to leave Clive gasping, conscious of how precarious his hold on her world was. In actual fact, however, a balance was always maintained: although Clive loved to feel on the brink, Vanessa never pushed him over.

In later life, his feeling for Vanessa was principally one of admiration that she could continue her professional life, her painting, without sacrificing her personal relationships. He never tired of her beauty and he appreciated her love for her children and her gift for organisation. He loved her for a depth which, when added to her tenderness and humour (even when not addressed to himself), gave her a distinction and mystery he never found elsewhere. In her youth, the mixture of a not unbarbed gaiety, a gentle and sometimes inspired irony, had been irresistible. Clive was not only a man of the world but a little boy, and much of Vanessa's charm lay in her ability to be discreetly maternal. If on her side this sentiment evaporated rather quickly, it was partly that it was impossible to continue loving a little boy as selfish as Clive, one who had never learned self-restraint, especially in sexual matters, and therefore lacked a sense of proportion. Neither had he, in spite of his knowledge and love of painting, any understanding of what it meant to be an artist: to him it was a mystery which he both loved and feared, because in Vanessa it was indissolubly linked to her femininity, her almost goddess-like capacity – as in the *Vénus d'Ille* – to love and to crush.

It was not only that Clive admired Vanessa's instinct for going her own way, he was also too lazy, perhaps too conscious of his own shortcomings, to stop her. He preferred her to shoulder the psychological problems of family life at the price of relinquishing his authority. It was perhaps his awareness of what was essentially an emotional failure that created in him a cold centre, a sterility which, for all his sociability and outward warmth, he could not completely conceal. And yet, though Clive suffered, his bitterness was addressed only to himself, never to her. For him she remained the only woman in whose house he could live with some semblance of contentment.

Between Clive and Duncan there was not the faintest shadow of jealousy – indeed it seems absurd to mention such a thing – and although this was no doubt largely because Duncan was a homosexual and that there was therefore no masculine rivalry, they also had a deep affection and understanding for each other. Clive, while he teased Duncan mercilessly for giving himself the airs of a colonel or major of some long-forgotten regiment, or for his almost uncritical catholicity of taste in art, or for any of his other idiosyncrasies, never patronised him, was always generous and never inconsiderate. It would have been only too easy for him to treat Duncan as an escaped lunatic or an *enfant terrible*, but this he never did. His respect for Duncan's personality was always evident, even if never directly spoken of. On his side, Duncan understood Clive and appreciated his sophistication, his erudition and the scope of his reading, which would often form the topic of their conversation. Neither had Duncan any prejudice against Clive's upper-class friends, with whom on occasion he was delighted to mix. He knew enough about them to enjoy Clive's reports of the latest intrigues and scandals, which often arrived at Charleston by letter, part of Clive's enormous correspondence. Often, Duncan's lightness of touch, and willingness to risk an original opinion, did more to cheer Clive than anything else. If Clive was the tinder, Duncan was the match, illuminating corners that would otherwise have been forgotten.

11

Bunny's Victory

My relations with my husband David Garnett had begun flirtatiously in 1936 or '37, when I was still at the London Theatre Studio, and had gathered in intensity until, in 1938, it had become a courtship – though not a love affair – about which I had very ambivalent feelings. I had known him all my life and had been to stay at Hilton Hall, his house in Huntingdonshire, where I met his wife, Ray, a sister of Frances Partridge, and her two small sons, Richard and William. Ray was quiet and still, very gentle; sitting before the open fireplace she asked me friendly questions, but as she always remained in the country I never got to know her well.

Bunny began to take me out to restaurants and theatres, for picnics in the country or to see his mother in her woodland cottage. He told me long stories to which I listened with hungry avidity: through them I caught glimpses of a vigorous mentality as well as of a life full, it seemed, of adventure – a life I longed to have experienced myself. In a continuous saga he exposed his own personality – or that part of it which he felt would create the best impression. I could hardly have been more gullible, whereas he, though appearing guileless, was certainly not without skill. He talked about his past – so very much longer than my own – and presented me with a youthful Corydon, unsophisticated, rash, adventurous and innocent, who attracted such people as D. H. Lawrence, Edward Thomas, H. G. Wells, and other writers whom, through him, I came to love. When he told me about his attempt to rescue the Indian political leader Savarkar from prison, I immediately saw him as another Rudolph Rassendyll, albeit without the aristocratic overtones. His visit to Russia as a boy of twelve, when he learnt the language by spending long days with the shepherds on the steppe, and his association with the revolutionary emigrés such as Prince Kropotkin and Sergei Stepniak, were incidents which seemed to connect me by a direct line with the world of the Russian novelists that I was just beginning to know. The fact that, when young, Bunny never had a penny in his pocket, went everywhere on foot or on bicycle, and was an only child, gave him the aura of the fool in the fairy story who always wins the princess in the end, either by fair means or foul.

He never disguised the fact that he had had many love affairs, though he left out those which might have touched me more nearly. As a child of Bloomsbury I took all this for granted, just as I felt it perfectly natural for him to make love to me while at home he had a wife and children. As it was he who took the initiative, I felt it was more his affair than mine – no other attitude occurred to me. I was already in the grip of a personality a hundred times more powerful than my own, in which I put far too much trust for the good of either of us. The accounts of his amorous exploits caused me no pangs of jealousy; his experience with the novelist Dorothy Edwards and his love affair with the artist's model Betty May – the tiger woman – were, for me, sealed in a past that was long over, packed away like a trunk in the attic. But as he opened it to take out a piece of crumpled brocade, with his slow speech, his evident strength of feeling and natural warmth, he had an unerring sense of the dramatic. He sat broad-shouldered in the lamplight, on his face a lop-sided smile; his blue eyes looking straight at and through me, deprived me of the ability to see that, under an urbane and charming exterior, Bunny was a bulldozer.

However intimately connected with Vanessa and Duncan, Bunny came from an entirely different background (although no doubt his grandfather, Richard Garnett, Keeper of Printed Books at the British Museum, knew Leslie Stephen). Bunny's parents, however, had no thought of being stars in the literary firmament, but belonged to its very core. They were less creative than professional, his mother a translator, his father a publisher's reader, both remarkable and highly intelligent people. They were hard working, frugal, blind to visual pleasures and indifferent to luxury.

Bunny, *c.* 1954

Edward Garnett, it is true, liked good wine, but Constance cared nothing for good food or any of the sensuous elements of life. In childhood she had suffered from a severe illness, had read a great deal, and eventually became one of the earliest women students at Cambridge. Later she taught herself Russian, and during her long life translated most of the Russian novelists. On at least one occasion she had smuggled information out of Russia and had befriended some of its political exiles: several settled near her in the woods overlooking the Sussex Weald, where she and Edward had built themselves a house. Here Constance worked and gardened for much of the time in solitude. Half-blind by the time I knew her, she nevertheless grew gentians in her garden, kneeling on the earth in order to see them, her face shaded by an old-fashioned sunbonnet.

Inside, the house was redolent of the Arts and Crafts Movement. The doors were of solid oak, with latches of ornamental wrought iron; the fireplaces were solidly constructed of hideous red brick; and everywhere there were gate-legged tables and woolwork embroidery. The floor was covered with slippery rugs or mats, and piles of ancient magazines stood in corners or disputed the black oak shelves with books of all shapes and sizes. The effect was of clutter and a disregard for visual harmony that I found painful. The lack of light and colour was oppressive, but Constance herself was delightful – guileless, bright, almost boyish, interested in everything in spite of her considerable age. She was also limpid and innocent, without *arrière pensée*. In spite of her acute mind and wide reading, she had no knowledge of the world and little of human nature: she was another example of a virginal temperament, although quite unworried by it.

One day early in our relationship Bunny invited Duncan and myself for the week-end to Hilton. As we drew up outside in his car, he turned round in his seat and surprised me with a long, sexy kiss, which Duncan in the back can hardly have avoided noticing. Bunny, although he had talked to me much of his years at Charleston in 1916–18, had been less than explicit about his love affair with Duncan – he was indeed never completely open about it. Neither had he told me that when I was born he had boasted that one day he would marry me. His kiss, though primarily addressed to me, was an unmistakeable warning to Duncan of his intentions, which it was a pity that Duncan ignored: Bunny, however, knew instinctively that he would. The place chosen was also significant, being within sight of the window from which Ray, at that moment, might be watching for our arrival.

She was already ill and Bunny was even then worried about her health. She had been operated on for cancer, and during the year 1938–39 her slow deterioration was always at the back and often in the front of his mind. His imaginative understanding of physical pain increased his distress, as did his guilt at the failure of their marriage, and the recognition that Ray had been, to a large extent, the victim of his own egotism. His appeal for sympathy as a repentant husband added to his attraction: he offered me a role in a tragic adult situation in which I had no responsibility. Ray was hardly real to me, and, although she was an object of genuine sympathy, I could not fail to realise that my youth and vitality were, in contrast, a strong attraction for Bunny.

The progress of our love affair was slow compared with Bunny's usual style with women; but he remained patient and tactful. There were many outings in London, some week-ends at Charleston, usually with the family, although on one occasion when we very much hoped to be alone, Vanessa and Duncan turned up at the last minute with the obvious intention of supervising us. Eventually I gave way to Bunny's insistence and lost my virginity, appropriately enough, in H. G. Wells's spare bedroom.

But however strong the physical attraction, I refused to say I loved him; I felt obscurely that real love was a different matter, and my heart was full of doubts which refused to disappear, although I could not put them into words. I was so inexperienced, so ignorant of myself, so doubtful whether I had any right to be listened to. The grown-ups, as I still thought of them, were lined up behind me waiting expectantly to see what I would do; and, at the time, I failed to recognise that Bunny belonged to their generation, not to mine. That was why, I later realised, no one of my own age had stood a chance beside him.

I was as putty in his hands, and many of his acts had a symbolic quality, as though he wanted to mould me into the sort of woman he needed. He took me to Ste Menehould in the north of France, where he had spent several months in the First World War working with the Quakers to rebuild the houses which had been destroyed. He stopped short of taking me to Ray's cottage at Swaledale in Yorkshire, much loved by her, but he drove me to Kettlewell nearby, where we enjoyed sardine picnics in the high, clear air, looking at the black-faced sheep and listening to the call of the curlew. After a slow start, I came to love the north every bit as much as he did. Although it was natural for him to want me to share his own enthusiasms, his behaviour was addressed as much to Duncan and Vanessa as to myself. It was very much as though he was saying to them, 'Stop me if you can!'

These moments of mixed happiness and anguish took place against a background of the Civil War in Spain and the growing certainty of a European war. In anticipation of this, Bunny had entered the Air Ministry, spending half the week in Fitzroy Street, where he had rented a room opposite my own, and the other half at Hilton. In the autumn I started going to the Euston Road School as an art student, but the following term was almost entirely taken up by an illness which, foolishly concealed, proved to be painful though not dangerous. As none of our bed-sitting rooms was suitable for an invalid, Bunny put me in a nursing home – a rather dramatic development which brought Vanessa to London in a state of intense anxiety. It would have been more tactful to put me to bed in her studio and call the family doctor, but Bunny realised how little I relished being nursed by Vanessa. He was in a difficult position in which nothing he did would have been acceptable to everybody; as it was, the episode made apparent the precarious nature of our family relations, underlining our inability to communicate with each other. I recovered, however, and all seemed to be well again.

Bunny's Victory

In September war was declared: we listened to Chamberlain on the radio in the garden at Charleston, which was glowing with the reds and oranges of the dying summer. The unreality of the occasion was in itself frightening, and yet there we all were – except for Julian – untouched and uncommitted, and seemed likely to remain so. As the suspension of hostilities continued throughout the autumn, so our sense of reality declined in direct ratio to the mounting tension: each day we expected and almost wanted something to happen, but were relieved when it did not.

The winter was cold, but the austerity of rationing had not yet begun; at Charleston we were comfortable enough. It was decided to celebrate my twenty-first birthday just before Christmas. Everyone was determined to make it a remarkable occasion, from Lottie, who slaved for a fortnight beforehand, to Vanessa, who thought of and organised it. Neither was I completely devoid of enterprise, since I had picked up a young German from Hamburg in the Charing Cross Road, where we were both looking at sheets of second-hand music. (When Bunny heard of his existence, mentioned in all innocence, he treated me to a devastating scene of jealousy with which I was ill-equipped to deal.) The young man was called Eribert; he was tall, thin and miserable, cut off from his country and hardly able to speak English. I invited him to my party, where he found himself in a situation rather like that of *Le Grand Meaulnes*, in a remote farmhouse full of people of all ages in evening dress, intimate and familiar, related to one another in ways that to him were a mystery. People's manners were free and easy, they were out to enjoy themselves; there was a defiant abundance of food and drink, and afterwards music and dancing. Every time Clive addressed Eribert, he rose to his feet, clicked his heels together and saluted. Much to Clive's credit, he did not bat an eyelid; he may indeed have enjoyed a politeness so unlike our own.

Eribert brought his flute and played it with Marjorie Strachey at the piano. She had not changed, remaining as fierce and vital as ever, delighted to be asked to a party for the young. She put on a garment of transparent purple held together at the back with a single brooch which, if it had come undone, would have revealed more than any of us were prepared for. After our supper of game pie and a good many glasses of wine, she set herself to entertain us with her star turn, the songs of 'Little Red Riding Hood' and 'Aiken Drum', whose britches were made of haggis bags. Her sense of humour was grotesque and achieved a lewdness I have never seen equalled, a ribaldry all the greater as none was meant, since these were nursery songs intended for children. Her appearance on these occasions was an asset; seedy, yellow-toothed, blowsy, like a wax candle melting in its socket, all her wit and vitality leapt into her small brown eyes, gleaming like polished boot buttons in her violently nodding head. Her finger wagged in admonishment, underlining the moral of the tale. Needless to say, her success was complete: we could not have enough of her and thought that everyone must feel the same. But poor Eribert was upset and terrified, and was finally discovered to have shingles, and so put to bed. Besides being the last party at Charleston, it was also his last moment of gaiety and civilisation before going to a camp for enemy aliens and thence to Canada, from where much later he sent me a postcard.

In the early spring Ray died, and Bunny took a farmhouse in the Weald, about five miles from Charleston. It must have been about this time, one day at Rodmell, that Virginia took me aside and asked me whether I was going to marry Bunny, implying that it would distress Vanessa very much if I did. At the time I had little thought of the future, a future threatened with the unknown caprices of war and social upheaval, and I said in good faith that I had no intention of it.

Meanwhile from our farmhouse we watched the Battle of Britain, seeing the Messerschmitts and Spitfires spiralling to earth as the smoke from their fuselage streamed upwards. In the air the planes were like toys, and it was hard to believe that the airmen manipulating them held our fate in their hands, so abstract seemed their performance from below. One evening Bunny mentioned an incident he had heard of, which involved shooting a German pilot on the ground after his plane had been shot down. The degree of Bunny's pleasure at this piece of so-called heroism shocked me intensely, not only as a reflection of the times we were living in but as a revelation of his own nature. To my protests he would only say that it was wartime and that I did not understand war. I could only stare at him and, thankfully, agree.

It was here at Claverham that I last saw Virginia, who with Leonard – and in spite of petrol rationing – came over to tea. With more than her usual insistence she clung to her 'rights', to which I reacted with more than my usual impatience. Perhaps I sensed a greater intensity than ever under her endearments, and for some reason could not respond with as much warmth as she would have liked – but then when could one ever have done so?

'Do you love me, Pixerina?'

'Of course I do, Virginia.'

Three days later I went down to the village to telephone to Charleston, and Clive told me she had disappeared, and was believed drowned. When, on returning to the house, I called out to Bunny, he put out his arms to embrace me with a warm bearlike gesture that in a crisis I learnt to expect from him.

At Charleston I found a fragile but not overwhelmed Vanessa: it must have been an event she had expected for most of her life, and now that it had happened it had lost its power to shatter. Virginia's death merely confirmed the general pessimism and sense of futility which surrounded us. On Duncan's arrival from London she broke the news to him, and we all three clung together in the kitchen, in a shared moment of despair, feeling that the world we knew, and the civilisation Virginia had loved, was rapidly disintegrating. Leonard, white from exhaustion, though as always objective and dispassionate, sat in the drawing-room and told us how they had found her body in the river, the river that Julian had loved, and where I could remember a dolphin that had once tempted Virginia down to the bank to stand beside us, watching its strange and lovely antics.

Bunny, who on Ray's death had been given compassionate leave from the Air Ministry, was now transferred to a secret propaganda department at Bush House. For the time being we lived in a service flat in Clifford's Inn. It was a new block, built between the wars, and predictably depressing. We felt like ants in an ant-heap making our way up innumerable stairs and down corridors to rooms like prison cells, where every evening we had difficulty in eliminating the shafts of light that came from our windows. This, and my methods of cleaning, rudimentary and unpredictable, eventually provoked the displeasure of the management, who regularly sent round a lady resembling a hospital matron to spy on its tenants. Our only relief was dining in the basement restaurant, where we were sometimes amused by the sight of Nancy Cunard carrying on with her lover at a nearby table.

It was in these hideous and claustrophobic surroundings that Bunny began to talk of marriage, a proposition which at first I firmly resisted. Now that I was living with him in London, Vanessa and Duncan's presence impinged on us far less than it had the year before, since they had become more or less settled at Charleston. Vanessa, who had always been in favour of a love affair, thought that marriage would be a fatal mistake. She foresaw responsibilities that she thought me unprepared for, as well as the sacrifice of my freedom to paint. She thought that Bunny at forty-eight was too old and that my feelings for him were unlikely to last; she was also afraid that I would suffer from his being something of a libertine.

She told me none of these things, however, emitting a vague feeling of worry and distress, the effect of which was to exasperate me. Her fears were not only for me but for Duncan, who had shown himself to be upset and jealous. Had the situation been less fraught with unavowed emotion, much of it impossible for me to understand, I might have felt free to enjoy my love affair without committing myself; but the feelings it provoked floated just beneath the surface, incomprehensible and menacing. Vanessa hovered in an anguish that I now find so easy to understand, holding long tête-à-tête conversations with Bunny. Her one

Myself, aged 19

desire was to protect both myself and Duncan, as it appeared, from life itself, when what I most needed was liberty and freedom. I should of course have asked questions; but I had been told the 'truth' so often that I thought I must know it. I had been brainwashed until I had no mind of my own. At the same time Duncan, Bunny and Vanessa were too closely bound together for there to be any room for me; the last thing they wanted was an illumination of the past, of the obscure corners they hoped to forget.

It is easy to see that both Duncan and Vanessa were suffering from a jealousy that would not have been so painful had my lover been of my own generation. Bunny was an intimate part of their past, and that he should step out of it and dare to claim their daughter as his wife seemed to them nightmarish, and utterly unjustifiable. Neither of them could tell us what they felt, partly because they were not prepared to put all their cards on the table, but also because Vanessa, in trying to protect first Duncan and then myself, only succeeded in preventing us from understanding each other. Traditionally speaking, it should have been Duncan's role as a father to rise in protest. But although Vanessa did get him to write a letter to Bunny, it had no effect – Bunny was deaf and dumb. I never saw the letter, but it is evident that Duncan's inadequacy arose from the fact that he did not feel like a father; how then could he behave like one? In addition, the intimacy between him and myself was too fragile to encourage my confidence, and a further complication was that my feelings for Bunny were essentially those of a daughter. How far Vanessa and Duncan understood this I am not sure: at any rate, they never found it possible to talk of it.

To many people it must have been obvious that my feeling for Bunny was not that of a wife, or wife-to-be; Maynard, for instance, appealed to him not to go on with the marriage. Bunny, however, had the bit between his teeth and not even Maynard's eloquence and authority could stop him. He was always immensely attracted by youth, drawing from it a strength which enabled him to remain young himself for an amazingly long time.

In some ways an excellent attitude, it was also a distortion, a failure to recognise the passage of time and its inevitable results. He was afraid of death, and – perhaps another facet of the same thing – afraid too of failure as an artist. He hoped that by marrying me he would take on a new lease of life.

It had never struck me as odd that Duncan, Bunny and Vanessa should have lived together during the years that preceded my birth. I had been brought up to think it perfectly natural, and, like Vanessa lacking in curiosity, I was not given to questioning the acts of the older generation. It would be only too easy for me now to see their situation in terms of sexual indulgence, jealousy and revenge though this is not how it appeared at the time, and may be over-dramatic. Perhaps it was natural that no one told me the one fact that seems to make sense of Bunny's behaviour: that he had proposed bed to Vanessa and had been rejected. Even though I now know this, I still find it hard to believe he was in love, since nothing he ever said pointed to more than a natural affection for her. But his affection coexisted with an unacknowledged resentment, and its only outlet lay in abducting her daughter.

When Bunny said at the cradle-side that he meant to marry me, no one took him seriously, it was so evidently an extravaganza disguised as a compliment, and neither Duncan nor Vanessa was in the habit of analysing other people's behaviour. But Bunny meant it literally, and did not forget it, and, knowing his nature, I find it impossible to believe that it was unconnected with jealousy, and perhaps with a desire to assimilate one who had been a part of both Duncan and Vanessa. Bunny longed to be loved, and to take possession of the loved one. If his insight into the workings of his own mind had not been obscured by egotism, Bunny might have realised what he was doing, since he could not be said to lack imagination. It seems clear enough now that when he carried me off to live as his wife and be a stepmother to his sons, his purpose was, at least in part, to inflict pain on Vanessa.

He knew also that he was driving a wedge between Vanessa and myself, one that in fact remained for ever. It was in this situation that Vanessa showed an almost saintly generosity, not only proving Virginia's early dictum true, but putting into practice the virtues of tolerance and forbearance so dear to Bloomsbury. It was hard for her to see her only daughter become a domestic slave, giving up, in practice if not in theory, any claim to the brilliant future Vanessa had hoped for. Bunny's egotism must have seemed unbelievably insensitive, as though he were stealing the single unequivocally successful result of her liaison with Duncan. Once more in the drawing-room at Charleston there was a scene between Vanessa and myself. She may have tried to tell me what her feelings really were, but became hysterical – an unnerving experience, which I could not face the risk of repeating. It is only now that I wonder what it was she was trying to tell me. My inadequacy as comforter, and my lack of the most rudimentary understanding, haunt me to this day.

Had I been a son things would have been very different, since I am sure Duncan would have had shown a much stronger interest in my existence. As a daughter, however, I was Vanessa's exclusive property, and as a female I was led to believe that I would need all the protection she could provide. Her strong desire to shield me was a partial atonement for what she felt she had deprived me of, and it caused me both annoyance and frustration. This is a fairly common experience between parents and children, but I had to deal with the entire weight of Vanessa's personality – difficult to resist as she was used to having the last word in all situations of importance.

Nor had I ever really allowed myself to realise how close Bunny and Duncan's relationship was from 1915 to 1918. I paid lip-service to the broad-mindedness of my parents, but I was shocked, not morally but physically, by the idea of homosexuality – a natural result perhaps of Duncan's lack of response to me – and I was unable to bring myself to think about it. Neither did I understand how incestuous my relationship with Bunny was. In the early months of our affair he suffered from moments of impotence, and must have realised something of the kind himself. Bunny also felt a guilt which he tried desperately to repress, and which, at the time, I saw no reason for. He attempted to justify his feelings with an intense and exalted romanticism which, allied to the character I had created for him of omnipotent father figure, was exactly calculated to disarm me. The story of our marriage could be summed up as the struggle on his side to maintain the unlooked-for realisation of a private dream, about which in spite of an almost wilful blindness, he must have had deep misgivings; and on mine the slow emancipation from a nightmare, which was none the less painful because I thought of it as almost entirely my own fault. Years later he would never admit that there was anything out of the ordinary in his love for the daughter of an old friend and her lover, with whom he had been so intimate. But he was never interested in the truth behind his feelings, only in their strength, which was for him their justification.

It is dangerous to talk only of people's secret motives, not only because one may so easily be wrong, but even more because they form but one strand among the many that make up a human being. Bunny, though I think he was actuated by selfishness, egotism and perhaps revenge – none of them attractive characteristics – and though this led him to make a victim of an ignorant and unsuspecting girl who was unable to defend herself, was not entirely a villain. As well as loving me for being Vanessa and Duncan's daughter, he loved me for myself, and in many ways he was singularly generous. Had I not married him, he would have been a perfect friend, one in whom I could have safely confided and who would always have given me good advice. When I eventually left him, although he was deeply hurt and never really recovered, he could not wish me ill: whatever he failed to understand he courageously tried to put up with.

In the end, Bunny's emotional determination overcame what had become a feeble and uncertain resistance. At bottom my love for him was simply a delusion – a dream which I had not the strength to sacrifice. Nevertheless, there was a moment when I thought of running away to a friend, but inertia, fear and ignorance prevented me. Seeing this, Bunny became even more urgent in his demands. He did not mean to be terrifying, but, like many people whose horizons are limited by a single, compelling objective, he was unaware of the impact he made. I saw myself being swept along by a dangerous current, but was unable to lift a finger to prevent it. An appeal to Vanessa would have saved me, but it was impossible to make: I preferred the unknown to the known, although I knew inwardly that I was doing the wrong thing.

We did not invite Vanessa and Duncan to the wedding, an omission which Quentin tried to repair. But we did not listen to his arguments, and I now see that it would have been impossible for Bunny to tolerate their presence at a ceremony which so flagrantly symbolised his victory. They were deeply wounded, and never afterwards alluded to what they probably considered as a piece of boorish stupidity.

The wedding took place at the substitute for the Guildhall, which had been bombed. We invited Frances and Ralph Partridge as our witnesses, together with my stepson William, who had just left school. I had on a too-short pink cotton dress and a straw hat more suitable for a woman of forty, into which I had pinned a rose. Standing in the small dreary room where the ceremony was held, I was for a moment almost overcome by panic: supposing, when the clerk asked for my consent, I said, 'No'? What a marvellous way out, what a simple solution! But I said, 'Yes', and the deed was done. I drowned my sense of guilt in champagne at the Ivy, Clive's favourite restaurant, where we had lunch. Then we caught the night train to Northumberland, where Bunny had just bought a small property.

Sadly and characteristically, neither Duncan nor Vanessa ever said a word to me of their disappointment: to them, such a thing would have been an act of unkindness, and they resolved to make the best of a bad job. Nevertheless, Bunny's relations with Duncan remained for many years chilly and distant, although with Vanessa he maintained an intimacy which was less stultified than my own, writing letters which enabled her to know more of me than I was aware of.

As for myself, I seemed unwittingly to have plunged into a

stagnant pool where nothing ever changed. My effort towards liberation from Vanessa had ended in a feeling of guilt and its concomitant paralysis. Although she was now over a hundred miles away, Vanessa was omnipresent: I still had not understood that some kind of confrontation was necessary – running away would solve nothing. With the birth of my children I undertook too many responsibilities, in an effort to disguise the fact that I was both lost and unhappy. Vanessa had always said, 'All I want is for you to be happy, darling,' – and now that I was not so, it seemed that the least I could do was pretend. As a matter of fact, I had never understood her anyway: it had always seemed to me that it was not happiness as such, but life that one wanted. What I had found, however, was not life, but a backwater, and I suppressed my unhappiness because I was ashamed of it. Little did I realise the poisonous nature of this attitude, nor how I was laying myself open to the traditional bugbear of the Stephens, masochistic self-pity, handed down, it seemed, from one generation to the next.

12

Nessa's Death

It was in 1944, when I was pregnant with my second daughter, that Vanessa discovered a lump in her breast, which she mentioned to me in a letter, telling me at the same time that she expected to be operated on almost immediately. I was in Yorkshire with Bunny when I received a telegram from Duncan to say that the operation had been successfully performed. No one called it a mastectomy or said it was cancer: the severity of the ordeal was submerged under a veil of stoicism and mystery. Vanessa must have suffered enormously from an experience for which in those days there was no psychological preparation and no support to be found from sharing it with others. For someone of her temperament this would in any case have been difficult, and she retired to the wartime austerity of Charleston rather as a wounded animal creeps into its lair, where Quentin's gentleness and Duncan's optimism may have done something to allay her natural anxiety. It was Vanessa's misfortune that at that time cancerous illnesses were regarded almost as though they were family scandals, to be brushed under the carpet; no one quite realised what she had been through, least of all myself. With the passing of time, however, she regained her strength, and salvation came to her through my children – she completely surrendered herself to their spontaneous affection.

By 1947 I had four daughters, the youngest twins. The years of their childhood gave me infinite pleasure – more than I can put into words. I felt and was very close to them, and at least one of them has told me that as a mother I was vivacious and full of gaiety. I certainly did not spend all my time moping about the failure of my marriage since, for one thing, I could not bear to admit that it was a failure. I was young and energetic, I loved country life, and, in addition to looking after my family, filled my time with projects of one kind and another. I continued to paint, to dressmake for myself and the children, to sing and play the piano and the violin, in what amounted to almost a fever of activity.

One of the reasons for my lack of emotional growth was the amount of hard work which I put into running my household. We lived in the same house in Huntingdonshire that Bunny and Ray had occupied when Duncan and I visited them before the war. Ray had left traces of her own personality on this charming seventeenth-century house, and the effect was so sensitive and fragile that I was afraid to touch it. It was only very gradually that, as walls and furnishings needed to be repainted or replaced, I felt free to impose my own more robust taste. We had little money and no luxuries, the house was unbelievably cold and draughty, our methods of heating antiquated, our supplies of hot water inadequate. For the first seven years of their lives the children were, it seemed, always ill, especially in winter.

It is true I had help, but as I refused to give up music and painting I was in a constant state of fatigue, and went to bed each night almost giddy with exhaustion. As I have said, a lot of this was unnecessary – a way of escaping thought and reflection. But it happens to many young mothers; once the extraordinary and irreplaceable experience of maternity has receded, one's horizon becomes limited to that of the children and one is temporarily incapable of further development. Even if there had been time to make new contacts I would have found it impossible to profit from them, and holidays offered only physical relaxation, not spiritual renewal.

Although Bunny was helpful and sympathetic, my dulled sensibilities only made our relationship less equal. In addition, there was social life. The house was often full of visitors: we had many friends in Cambridge as well as in the village, and, seeing my life through their eyes, I built up an image of myself as the perfect young mother-housewife-hostess, and spent much of my energy living up to it. The only drawback – and it was a very serious one, symptomatic of what lay underneath – was my growing misunderstanding with Bunny, and his shattering rages, which, disconcertingly and tragically, often included the children.

If it is true to say that it was because of them that I stayed with Bunny, it is not an excuse I defend; those disposed to indulgence will sympathise with my doubts about how to bring up four children on my own when I was unqualified for any profession. But I know that, had I had the courage, it would have been possible to separate earlier, and it might have done the children less harm to live precariously with me than to stay as they did with parents who were obviously and increasingly unhappy together. It was Bunny who would have suffered, and would have both reproached and tormented me, and it was this more than the unknown future that was for me the stumbling block. If I ever had to justify my own point of view, my reasoning turned to jelly, my defences into men of straw. Confused and doubtful even when my emotions were strong, how then could I persuade Bunny to accept my departure? And to depart without his consent – knowing that my children were also his – seemed to me an utter impossibility. But I did not try – and perhaps I am unjust to him.

Perhaps it was because of Bunny's greater emotional power, or the contrast of my own youth and inexperience, but I came to think of him as 'impervious'. He had made up his mind about a lot of things and thought he *knew the truth*. He entrenched himself in what he knew he felt: his emotions were not spontaneous, but often whipped into a paroxysm of feeling. His sincerity lay in the desire to prove his feelings genuine, and I felt embarrassed to see him writhing in the effort, rather than just letting the emotion itself run through him.

In early days I was swept off my feet by Bunny's concern for me: never had I experienced anything of the kind, except for certain brief moments with Julian. Either I was blind to his excess or, having been deprived of displays of feeling, I hungered for them. When we were man and wife, however, I gradually became repelled by his emotionalism, which always seemed just off the mark. I became afraid it would distort my own emotions, and took to keeping them more and more to myself. I began to imitate Vanessa's habit of reserving her most precious feelings to herself, and appeared far colder and more critical than I really was; and this to Bunny was anathema.

This was only one of the tortuous ways in which our misunderstanding grew, almost as though it had a will of its own. We had both sinned not only against each other but against ourselves, and were suffering for it. Had I had the courage to face my own feelings, I might perhaps have faced Bunny. We might have arrived at a *modus vivendi*, or I might have left him sooner than I did. For me, age and authority were great obstacles. It was obvious that I needed help but I did not know how or where to find it, and I was almost as afraid of help as I was of everything else.

During my entire marriage my relation to Duncan and Vanessa remained far too close. I saw them whenever I went to London and, when it again became possible after the war, we often went abroad together. Incestuously bound up with each other, we found each other's company more familiar, less exacting and, by the same token, less stimulating than anyone else's. For me there seemed to *be* no one else; domesticity put me out of bounds on the one hand, and on the other my close association with my parents hedged me round with invisible barriers.

In spite of my inability to keep away from them, my relation with Vanessa had not changed, and was as negative as ever. When I visited Charleston, I would sit with her by the studio stove, unable to utter a word. Neither of us knew what was wrong: we were submerged by inertia and depression. I do not know what prevented me from taking the initiative, why I did not think of asking questions, of opening up the past – and with this way blocked, there was no other. It is true that when she did talk she continued to 'poke fun'; her irony was unquenchable. But although it was amusing it was defensive, and barred the way to deeper emotional exchange. I was painfully conscious of an undercurrent of thought, the masochistic nature of which repelled me. I was still too young, too egotistical also, to sympathise with an attitude in which all I saw was a refusal to participate in the more vital aspects of life. With too great a facility we attributed Vanessa's chronic melancholy to the death of Julian; but although this had dealt her a gigantic blow, I felt that it had brought out something in her that had always been there, of which I had been conscious even as a child. I knew that Vanessa was longing for a demonstration of love – like Virginia though, unable to ask for it frankly – while on my side my feelings were frozen. The key to emotion was lost; we both sat there like flies in amber, impotent.

Amongst ourselves, Vanessa often gave way to the temptation of self-denigration, applying it, not without reason, to her own appearance, but far more distressingly to her painting. I never heard her say she was pleased and proud of something she had done, and the effect of this attitude was demoralising. It was directly opposed to the side of her which insisted on being right, and it was disconcerting to realise that, although she felt morally certain of being able to control other people's lives, she was in a state of confusion about her own. In talking about her work she was really talking about herself, and her despairing statements about the inferiority of her painting were one interminable question addressed to Duncan who, though he may well have understood its nature, was in no position to satisfy her. She longed for recognition not so much as a painter but as a woman, and this he could not give her.

According to Paul Roche, in 1918, the year of my birth, Duncan had told Vanessa that he felt incapable of having further sexual relations with her. Thus her victory, if it was one, in keeping Duncan for herself was at best pyrrhic, gained at a cost she failed to assess. She seems to have accepted it as a necessary sacrifice for the privilege of living with this immensely attractive yet incomplete human being, to whom she was so passionately attached, and there must have been a strong element of masochism in her love for him, which induced her to accept a situation which did permanent harm to her self-respect. In other words,

Vanessa, 1951

she lost sight of herself as a valid individual. By the time I am speaking of, their relationship, though deeply affectionate, was lop-sided, even though it appeared justified by years of habit. Vanessa, having allowed herself to suffer at Duncan's hands, was compelled to idolise him in order to vindicate the loss of her physical fulfilment: had he been less of a genius the sacrifice would not have been worth it. She gained companionship with a man she loved on terms unworthy of her whole self, infinitely damaging to her pride. Whereas Duncan remained young and vital, she became old for her years and fixed in her attitudes.

It is tempting to wonder whether, if Vanessa had known what she was doing to herself, she would have acted differently. In her picture 'The Tub', painted in 1918 and now in the Tate Gallery, there is a young woman standing stark naked and alone by a tub of water, which is I feel sure a self-portrait symbolising not only loneliness but a moment of truth and self-questioning. It suggests that she was aware of having reached a crisis, and through her painting was calling for help. She put the painting away, and for many years it lay in the attic, as though the situation it recalled was too disturbing to be contemplated.

I was always puzzled by the difference between her painting during the war and that which followed. Part of the reason for both her and Duncan's change of style was to be found in their natural reaction to a profound difference in the quality of life itself, but in Vanessa's case a greater maturity seemed to be accompanied by a lessening not only of self-confidence but of vitality. The remarks of her less sensitive friends, confusing her work with Duncan's, were not without percipience; instead of standing on her own, she now seemed to lean for her inspiration on him. Her compensation for this loss of autonomy lay in his love for her as a mother figure, his trust in her, and their mutual sympathy over painting, which, as far as her consciousness went, were enough. His charm and magic never palled or became stale; he remained the apple of her eye.

In her own quiet and concentrated way Vanessa found much to enjoy, and it was perhaps her grandchildren, in whom she had no vested interest, who brought out her most human and delightful qualities. She spoiled them outrageously – the prerogative of grandmothers. She left in the minds of my two elder daughters, inevitably those who knew her best, the memory of deep affection and humour. She read aloud to them, as she had to me, and having as a result of long wartime evenings taken to knitting, a tube of brightly striped sock grew slowly longer and longer; when she reached the end of a round or a page there was always a moment of doubt as to whether knitting would take precedence over reading, or vice versa. Her steel needles moved slowly in and out, exploring their way through each stitch, coaxed rather than flicked by her long sensitive fingers. An eternal spiral descended into her lap, produced almost unconciously: what she was making seemed hardly to concern her – she resembled the Goddess of Earth eternally reproducing the symbol of creation.

As she read, her spectacles would slip to the end of her nose while she ran her eye along the page, ready at the same time to catch any sign of restlessness on the part of the children. Her voice, grave and cool, rising and falling monotonously, hypnotised and calmed her listeners.

From Charleston, Vanessa maintained a loving correspondence with my children, her notepaper covered with drawings of cats, goldfish and little girls, while the post often contained parcels of finished socks and other small presents. There were also outings to the zoo and the theatre which, in spite of inevitable exhaustion, she enjoyed immensely. With age she had become thinner and more bent, dressing in clothes of grey and iron black. She had never dressed in the same way as other people; her clothes had always been defiant of convention and since middle age they had become increasingly unrelated to her own beauty. Whether she realised it or not, they were a further expression of her disappointment in herself. She had never indulged in, or more probably could never be bothered with, the refinement and elegance of a Mary Hutchinson or an Ethel Sands, but then her physical splendour had always been there, whether she paid it attention or not. Now in age her clothes seemed to say with dignified finality: 'You must take me as you find me.'

Despite looking a little reminiscent of a peasant woman minding a herd of goats, she emanated distinction. Her movements were slow and tentative, her manner enquiring but impressive. In the Charleston dining-room she presided over the table painted by herself; it was round, but where she sat was the indubitable head of it. There she ruled for forty years, dispensing food with measured precision and increasing frugality. In front of her stood the joint of cold beef from which day after day she cut a few grey slices, while at the bottom of the salad bowl there lurked some leaves of lettuce, and in the pewter dishes which Julian had brought back from China there were hardly enough sprouts and potatoes to satisfy our appetites – not that we actually suffered from hunger, but the old prodigality had withered. The meal always ended with her making coffee, of which the concentrated drops, like some alchemic potion, fell one by one into the pot. Without seeming aware, we all watched her lift the heavy kettle and tilt it, allowing just the right amount of boiling water to fall on the coffee grounds, from which a cloud of steam arose with a hiss like some tame serpent. This had always been for me the perfect cadence at the end of a meal, the resolution towards which all the events of the morning converged, ushering in the withdrawn privacy of the afternoon.

One of Vanessa's principal pleasures, as always, was to go abroad. Anticipating what they called adventure, she and Duncan would pack up their painting things and go to Venice, Lucca, or Perugia in Italy, or to Auxerre or other small places in France where, installing themselves in some modest pensione or auberge, they would immediately set out to find a subject. There was no nonsense about absorbing the atmosphere or taking time to settle down: they started a sketch at once by church or riverbank, afterwards enjoying a sedentary evening in a café and supper eaten on the terrace, recounting in amused and rather exclusive accents the events of the day. Vanessa visibly relaxed in this atmosphere, enjoying from a chosen distance the warmth of the Italians or the vitality and common sense of the French. When I could, I joined them on these holidays. It was easier to talk to Vanessa abroad; freed from her usual commitments she was livelier, and a thousand small things distracted us from the problem of our own relationship.

Our deepest emotions were called out by the beauty that surrounded us. An October visit to Venice was crowned by a day spent in the autumnal timelessness of Torcello, and another crossing the lagoon to Chioggia, where after a day's sketching we returned in the dark, mesmerised by the sails of the fishing boats caught in the lights of our small steamer, swelling like pale moths on the dark water. I remember another holiday on the Yonne at a small inn, the patron of which had been an active member of the resistance. He was an enthusiastic admirer of the English as well as a skilled raconteur, reminding me a little of Michel, and telling us story after story about blowing up trains or receiving parachutists in the woods at night. Through Bunny I knew something of General Buckmaster and had met one or two of the agents who had been dropped in France, and was therefore, with Duncan, genuinely interested; but Vanessa remained aloof, either from an intense dislike of war, or from an inability to sympathise with the active, extrovert side of life.

The last of these holidays was as late as 1960, when Vanessa and Duncan rented the Bussys' house, La Souco, in Roquebrune near Mentone. This time they were not in a hotel but in a home from home, accompanied by Grace to do the cooking. I had last seen the house when I was seventeen, and it held for me potent memories of Dorothy Bussy, Lytton Strachey's sister, hunched in an armchair reading, her straight grey hair falling over her spectacles, occasionally regarding me with a look of intelligent sympathy. Her husband, Simon, was like a little owl, fierce and stubborn. It was he who did the housekeeping, scolding the cook without mercy for such culinary *faux pas* as putting too much salt in the salad – I seem to remember that it was a fault she committed rather too often. Simon was taciturn but vital, concentrating on his painting in secrecy in his studio at the back of the house. He was now dead, and Duncan, Vanessa and I looked amongst the piles of his paintings, pastels and drawings disintegrating under the skylight. They were the record of a passionate but solitary nature; he had left behind him early works of imaginative grandeur which, shrinking gradually to smaller proportions, could at times be singularly sensitive and beautiful.

The saffron walls and white curtains, though shabbier, were unchanged, as were the innumerable paperbound books covering the walls of the staircase. Outside, the garden fell away to the sea far below in terraces dotted with olive, orange and lemon trees on which the fruit hung like small lanterns. The paths, though full of weeds, were bordered with miniature blue irises, and, looking upwards, one could see the cinnamon-coloured houses of the village against a violet sky.

We had a car, which Duncan drove with inspired irresponsibility into Mentone for lunch with Clive and Barbara Bagenal, who were as usual staying there for the winter; or else we went up into the hills to find a subject to paint. Vanessa no longer drove; she was becoming very stiff and slow with rheumatic knees, causing her considerable pain of which she never complained. She had become forgetful, failing uncharacteristically to order lunch or doing so twice over. More and more often she would nod off to sleep in her chair. Duncan was worried by these signs of failing powers, and, as was his way, became stubborn and crotchety; I often found myself in sudden disagreement with him about nothing, which dismayed Vanessa. None the less the mood was a happy one, enlivened by the sophisticated presence of Clive and Barbara and by the exquisite weather, which for the moment seemed as though it would continue for ever.

On their return to England, Duncan and Vanessa continued every fortnight to spend two or three nights in London at Percy Street, where they now had Saxon Sydney-Turner's old rooms. One night they gave a dinner party for a couple of old friends, when Vanessa fell into a dead faint and could not be brought round. Duncan called the ambulance from the Middlesex Hospital. Once there, she revived and immediately protested that she was perfectly well, insisting on going home at once. Characteristically, she decided to say nothing to me, and I only knew of the incident from Michel Saint-Denis after her death.

In the winter of 1960 she became seriously ill in Percy Street with pneumonia. The flat was inconveniently placed at the top of the house and suddenly seemed poorly equipped and squalid. When the worst was over and Vanessa was a little stronger, she was driven down to Charleston. Clearing up after her departure, I was shocked by the dirty sheets, the dust on furniture and floors, the filth in the kitchen. It brought home to me Vanessa's age and her growing incapacity, disguised so far by her determined independence: later I realised that this was a happy state of affairs rather than otherwise, since it implied that she had remained in command very nearly until the end.

In the spring of 1961 Clive was ill in the London Clinic. Late one afternoon he telephoned me at Hilton: Vanessa had again developed pneumonia and was not expected to live through the night. I took the first train from Huntingdon, crossed London in a taxi, and just caught the train to Lewes. Although it had been obvious for some time that Vanessa was failing, the thought that she might die was unbelievable, terrible and at the same time inadmissibly exhilarating. Like the disappearance of some familiar monument, her absence would reveal a new perspective in which I might be able to find freedom. It was thus that my thoughts ran, or rather burst to the surface like bubbles from a stagnant pool, as I sat in the train.

Taking a taxi from the station, I arrived at Charleston to find Duncan and Quentin in a state of shock, though perfectly calm. Duncan, in whose eyes there were tears, took me to Vanessa's ground-floor bedroom, which looked onto the garden: she had died only an hour before. She was lying on her bed, white but austerely beautiful. Duncan suggested that I should do a drawing of her – but of this I was quite incapable. He did one himself, which I still have.

I was puzzled by the fact that I had not even known that Vanessa was unwell. Why had not Duncan, instead of Clive, telephoned me? The more I thought of it the more stunned and the more excluded I felt, especially when I realised that her illness had lasted for about ten days. My eldest daughter, then eighteen, and Quentin's son Julian had both been there, only sent away the very day I arrived. Possibly no one had realised how close Vanessa was to death. Quentin apologised for having said nothing; there had apparently been some mistake. But no real explanation was forthcoming, and I accepted, too easily, a failure that hurt me deeply.

Vanessa was buried in Firle churchyard, her only mourners Duncan, Quentin, myself, and Grace and her husband, Walter. There is now a stone there giving her dates: 1879–1961. Oddly enough, it was difficult to believe she was eighty-one, in spite of the fact that she had always seemed such an elderly mother. So unalterable had she always appeared that I could not imagine the world without her, especially that private world of her own which she had created as a refuge from outsiders and as a haven for her family – the world in which she had nurtured us all both to our confusion and our delight.

I stayed on at Charleston; already my relations with Duncan were becoming more intimate. He was, I believe, very miserable, but did not talk much about Vanessa. One day after his death, on looking through some drawings, I found a small piece of paper dated June 3rd, 1961, written in his unmistakable handwriting.

After lunch I suddenly became aware that I am now 'on my own' for better or worse.

Exactly what I mean? I can only guess by using the word 'deference' that is what I always felt with V. I do not mean the suggestion of flattery which the word has, but I always did defer to her opinions and feelings. Now henceforth I think I shall always defer to her opinions, I know or can guess so often what they would be – but her feelings no longer exist, so in that respect I feel I am alone.   D.G.

The transparency of this small document is for me like a testimony to the quality of their relationship; its ingenuousness is touching, reminding me of an offering, not to Vanessa herself so much as to the gods, of fresh herbs picked at dawn. These feelings were struggling to express themselves during those long days spent in the studio, before he started to work again. One evening Clive arrived back from the nursing home and, sitting exhausted in his downstairs book-room after the journey, gave way to a greater emotion than I had ever seen him show before. The world for him would be an infinitely poorer place without Vanessa, and Charleston itself without her was but a pale reflection of what it had been. Until Duncan regained his balance we all lived in suspension. No outward habits were changed, but the *raison d'être* of the old ones had vanished.

EPILOGUE

Short as it is, this book has taken me seven years to write. To a professional author this must seem ridiculous, but to me it represents nothing so much as an emergence from the dark into the light.

In fact I was beginning to burst the bonds many years before Frank Hallman suggested that I should write a book. I owe my eventual emancipation from Bunny's domination to a chance contact with the works of Karen Horney, a Freudian psychologist. Something in me responded to her writing, and I was conscious that I had found one of the keys to freedom, although, still suffering from timidity, my progress was erratic and ill-informed. Later, I was galvanised by one of my daughters, who not only had her own problems but a very clear idea of what she wanted. Her crisis had a deep emotional impact and brought me to life – it also taught me much; but I have learnt precious lessons from all my children.

At about the same time that I made up my mind to leave Bunny, I, like Vanessa, had to have a mastectomy. It was a devastating experience, and I knew then what she must have suffered. If I mention it now, it is only to say that I am convinced it was a result more of my unhealthy state of mind than of my body. Luckily for me, it seems to have been in the nature of a warning, which even then I was beginning to heed.

It is generally believed that to understand all is to forgive all, but apart from the fact that it is impossible to understand everything, to talk of forgiveness smacks too much of superiority. Understanding is enough – if one can achieve it – but there is no doubt it comes and goes. There are moments when I feel hard done by, and others when I recognise that Vanessa meant me no harm. It was a sin of omission; and although those are the sins that have the worst effect, they are the ones which must – there is no way of avoiding the word – be forgiven. Writing this book has in itself made me try to understand, and I can say now, with untold relief, that I am more able to see Vanessa through other people's eyes.

Not long ago I was sorting out the family photographs, nearly all taken by Vanessa. I thought I knew them well enough and that the job would be merely mechanical, but I found it highly emotive and disturbing, particularly in relation to my book. What had I said? What picture had I drawn and how true was it? How did it compare with this assembly of black-and-white images stuck to the page, rather like the keys of an old piano whose notes tinkle suggestively in the stale air of memory? Their message is one of happiness and enjoyment: they convey so much better than the written word the moments of vitality that have receded, leaving in their wake a world of shadows.

To me no one appears more shadowy than myself, or more questionably portrayed in my book. I was not completely solitary, lonely and withdrawn. On the contrary, I was often full of high spirits, I teased others as they teased me, I danced and laughed. I was given pleasure and I returned it, but there remained the hidden side of myself.

I now see my childhood as a precarious paradise, slung like a cradle over a cloud, but none the less full of delight. And yet it seems to me that one's maturity should be a better time than one's childhood, however wonderful that may have been. Mine has only just begun. Although retarded by some thirty years or more, it is still worth having, but in the effort to gain it I may have painted Vanessa in darker colours than she merited, having no doubt distorted her for my own purposes. In the nature of things, however, an autobiography cannot pretend to be objective. I have tried to describe my own ghosts, and, in doing so, to exorcise them.

Index

Index

feelings, 55; reading, 56, 74, 139; knocked down by car, 62; early curiosity about sex, 65, 121–3, 125, 139; sacrifices dolls, 75–6; schooling, 77–8, 80, 86, 114; portraits, 79, 91, 98, 102, 112, 153; appearance, 84; love and playing of music, 86–7, 116–17, 125, 161; visits to theatre, 88; learns of parentage, 89, 134–6; stage ambitions, 116; learns Italian, 116; character and emotional life, 122–3, 136, 163; in Paris, 124–5; at London Theatre Studio, 126–7, 132; marriage, 135, 157–8, 160–3; David Garnett courts, 143–4, 146–8, 152, 154–7; studies art, 148; children, 160–2; painting, 161; mastectomy, 175

Garnett, Constance, 144, 146

Garnett, David ('Bunny'): lives in France, 1; AG leaves, 1, 175; on Vanessa, 13; relations with Duncan Grant, 36, 39, 146–7, 154–6, 158; on birth of Vanessa's children, 38; as Conscientious Objector in Great War, 39; and AG's childhood, 52; on Duncan Grant's parents, 67; criticises AG's disdain of others, 85; flies aeroplane, 100; and Julian's death, 132; courts AG, 143–4, 146–8, 152, 154–7; marriage to Ray, 143, 147; background, 144, 146; portrait, 145; jealousies, 149, 155; in World War II, 150–2; marriage to AG, 158, 161–2

Garnett, Edward, 144, 146

Garnett, Fan (AG's daughter), 8, 10

Garnett, Ray (David's 1st wife), 143, 147, 149, 161

Garnett, Richard (David's son), 143

Garnett, Richard (David's grandfather), 144

Garnett, William (David's son), 143

Gordon Square, London: no. 46, 48–55; no. 50, 138

Grace (maid), 41, 54, 65, 71–2, 92, 169

Grant, Major Bartle (Duncan's father), 38, 66–7

Grant, Duncan (AG's father): AG's relations with, 2–5, 121, 123, 128–30, 135, 137, 156, 163, 172; life at Charleston, 3–4, 7, 92–3; 93rd birthday, 8; death, 9–10; and Virginia Woolf's jealousy of Vanessa, 22;

relations with Vanessa, 28, 32–5, 39, 94–5, 129–30, 164–6, 172; background, 33; personality and character, 33–5, 109, 128–9; homosexuality, 33, 36; portrait, 34; as Conscientious Objector in Great War, 35, 39; relations with David Garnett, 36, 39, 146–8, 152, 154–6, 158; children, 37–8; and Charleston garden, 45; AG sees naked, 49; decorates Virginia Woolf's London home, 53; typhoid, 65–6; parents, 66–7; at La Bergère, 67–9; and AG's Cuckmere escapade, 76; music, 87; stage designs, 88; paintings, 94–5, 103, 166; and Helen Anrep, 100; making things, 101; in Rome, 117; decorates *Queen Mary*, 117; virginal quality, 122; in Fitzroy Street, 127–8; and Julian's death, 132; AG learns of fatherhood, 134–7; relations with Clive Bell, 141–2; and Virginia Woolf's death, 151; and AG's marriage, 158; and Vanessa's illness, 160; later trips abroad, 168–9; and Vanessa's death, 171–2

Grant, Ethel (Duncan's mother), 38, 65–7, 87

Hallman, Frank, 2, 7, 175

Ham Spray (house, Wiltshire), 99

Hammersley, Mrs (pianist), 128

Harland, Mr & Mrs (Keynes's cook and husband), 50–1

Henderson, Sir Nicholas, 9

Hills, Jack, 23, 25–6

Hills, Stella (née Duckworth), 16–18, 21, 23; portrait, 20

Hilton Hall (Huntingdonshire), 143, 146, 161

Hodgkin, Frances, 81

Hogarth Press, 53

Honey, Dorothy (née Bell; Clive's sister), 56–7, 59–61

Horney, Karen, 175

Hutchinson, Mary, 167

Italy, 115–18, 168

Jackson, Julia *see* Stephen, Julia

Keynes, John Maynard, Baron, 15, 39, 48, 130, 132, 154

Index

Index

Walpole, Hugh, 110
Walter, François, 124–5
Walter, Zoum (wife of François), 125–6
Wells, H. G., 143, 147
Whistler, James McNeill, 128
Woolf, Leonard: in Sussex, 39; in Tavistock Square, 52; relations with AG, 53, 106, 108–9; character, 106–8; at Charleston, 107–8; plays bowls, 110–11; relations with wife, 113–14; virginal quality, 122; and Virginia Woolf's death, 151
Woolf, Virginia: fame, 15; family, 16; personality, 19; relations with Vanessa, 19–22, 27, 107–8, 111; portraits, 20, 112; upbringing, 21; breakdowns, 22, 113–14; creates character for Vanessa, 22–3; flirts with Clive Bell, 26–8; in Sussex, 39; in Tavistock Square, 52–4; AG's childhood visits to, 53; at Charleston, 106; relations with AG, 106–7, 110, 113–14, 151; at Rodmell, 110–11; gives dress allowance to AG, 111; relations with husband, 113–14; appearance, 113; virginal quality, 113, 122; flirtations with women, 131; and Julian's death, 132; and David Garnett's courtship of AG, 150; suicide, 151
World War II, 149

Yeats, W. B., 80
Yonge, Charlotte M., 56, 74